AERIAL
2011

John Glenn's Fine Arts Magazine

John Glenn High School
201 John Glenn Drive
Walkerton, Indiana 46574
Enrollment: 611
Volume 28

CREATIVE SPARKS

"A thought often makes us hotter than a fire." - Henry Wadsworth Longfellow

"My imagination completely controls me, and forever feeds the fire that burns with dark red light in my heart." - Kim Elizabeth

Sparks Fly

Poetry Renga by Emily Thomas, Senior;
Autumn Ladyga, Senior; and Kate Carlson, Senior
Charcoal by Ayla Felix, Senior

My paint on a brush
strokes a clean canvas;
fingers on the keys of a saxophone
make melody. My happiness.

My eyes on a book:
the ideas are blazing,
my thoughts are spinning,
the pencil is racing. My passion.

My ideas pour from my mind
in a white hot heat
in a cloudburst of cold sweat.
My life, my creative life.
Let the sparks fly.

CREATIVE SPARKS
2011

AuthorHouse™
1663 Liberty Drive
Bloomington, IN 47403
www.authorhouse.com
Phone: 1-800-839-8640

First published by AuthorHouse 3/18/2011

ISBN: 978-1-4567-5594-2 (sc)
ISBN: 978-1-4567-5593-5 (e)

Printed in the United States of America

PATRONS
FUEL FOR THE FIRE

Platinum
Falcon 500 Club
Tri-Kappa Epsilon
Deborah Sullivan Brown,
Attorney

Gold
Don & Sandy Thomas
1st Source Bank
Miller's Merry Manor
Teacher's Credit Union
Starke County Farm Bureau
Co-operative

Bronze
Animal Hospital of North Liberty
Barry's Photography
Bob's Country Store
Center Street Video
Just for You
Kabelin Ace Hardware

Boosters
Allsop Farms
Judy Allsop
Robert Allsop
Sue & Al Allsop, Allsop Construction
Chuck's Barber Shop
JF New Native Plant Nursery
John Small Insurance
Kayla Goforth
Kevin Dosmann
Mark O'Brien
Ronda Wade
Sara Rippy
Tangles Hair Salon
The Kitchen Store
The Yum-Yum Shoppe

AERIAL STAFF
FIRESTARTERS

editors Megan Beery, Kate Carlson, Chantell Cooper, and Autumn Ladyga

art editor Emily Thomas

editorial staff Thomas Adamson, Megan Beery, Kirsten Brown, Kate Carlson, Ariel Clark, Chantell Cooper, Nick Havranek, Lina Hennig, Jacob Hoyt, Olivia Hurley, Chloe Jacobson, Abby Johndrow, Emily Kensinger, Autumn Ladyga, Jenna Luczyk, Kelsey Mitschelen, Christina Newhart, Cody Phillips, Mariah Rippy, Cristina Rudynski, Emily Thomas, and Danielle Wroblewski

design and layout Kirsten Brown, Kate Carlson, Nick Havranek, Chloe Jacobson, Autumn Ladyga, and Mariah Rippy

art advisors Mr. John Thomas and Mrs. Amy Hughes

aerial **and literary advisor** Mr. Paul Hernandez

administration Superintendent Richard Reese
Principal Will Morton
Assistant Principal Chris Winchell

printers AuthorHouse
1663 Liberty Drive, Suite 200
Bloomington, Indiana 47403
Adalee Cooney, Assistant Manager, Production

"The instructions we find in books are like fire.
We fetch it from our neighbors, kindle it at home, communicate it to others,
and it becomes the property of all." Voltaire

CONTENTS
FLASHPOINTS

CONTENTS

artwork

CONTENTS

CAMPFIRE LIGHT

"So like a forgotten fire, a childhood can always flare up again within us." - Gaston Bachelard

Bask in the warm glow of childhood, memories, and growing up...

Wasn't It Wonderful

Poetry Renga by Lina Hennig, Junior;
Nick Havranek, Junior; Danielle Wroblewski, Senior;
and Megan Beery, Senior
Oil by Kimberly Lord, Junior
Scholastic Art Award Silver Key

We should just pretend
that everything was well
with holding hands and good night kisses.
That would be a wonderful day,
Our wonderful day.

We would play together,
always knowing what we
could never tell. These thoughts roam,
and we cheat and steal and lie.
Our wonderful lies.

We would share stories,
while being entangled in each other's grasp,
but now your arms seem so cold,
and I haven't felt your
heartbeat in awhile.
Our wonderful hearts.

We could be great explorers
in a tent made of sheets,
Your laugh and my smile,
neither have been here in quite awhile.
I miss the way we were,
the wonderful way we were.

White Curtains

Poetry Renga by Danielle Wroblewski, Senior;
Christina Newhart, Senior; Cody Phillips, Junior
and Emily Thomas, Senior
Photo by Kate Smith, Senior

A warm summer breeze fills
the room, ruffling white cotton
curtains. The smells of lilac and
sunshine grace my senses like
past Julys in bloom.

In my mind, I'm sitting outside,
and I smell roses while I bask
in the sunshine and
listen to the waves hitting
against the rocks below.

Feeling euphoric for
I am only four,
nobody is bothering me,
and if they were, I'd simply
ignore them.

I'm in Mommy's arms
as we watch the tide roll in and recede.
She sees my shining face and we giggle.
I'm young again for a moment more,
until the curtains shock me to reality.

Lily Pad Monsters

Nonfiction by Ayla Felix, Senior
Scholastic Writing Award Gold Key
Photo by Kate Smith, Senior

I used to live in Koontz Lake. Well, not the actual lake, because no one lives *in* a lake, but I used to live within easy walking distance of the lake. Up until seventh grade, anyway. I loved going down to the lake every day during summer vacation and on weekends, even when it was too cold to go swimming. I met some really amazing people there, and got to see some interesting things. There's nothing like a throng of strangers to get you to see the truths, both beautiful and ugly, about human nature.

I was nine, and it was hot. So unbearably hot that I didn't really *want* to go to the lake, because it was too hot to move, but the neighbors weren't home, and my brother was being annoying. So I got permission and walked to the lake, towel over my shoulder and big bucket on my arm. There were a lot of people at the beach that day—more than there had been all summer. Mostly adults and really little kids, but there were some other nine-year-olds, too. I didn't know any of them, but that wasn't new. Every summer I made new transient friends that I never saw again.

I put my towel under the lone willow on Crehmer's Beach, and left my sandals and bucket there, too. I didn't think anything would be stolen, and even if something was, they were cheap sandals, an older beach towel and

a plastic bucket. Easily replaced, though I never thought of that. All I thought of was the lake, cool and amazing after the heat. I plunged right in.

I never swam out too far. I was a good swimmer, but not the best, and farther out the seaweed grew tall enough to tangle your legs. That and I still had some little kid fear left over from the stories my teenage relatives would tell me about the "lake monsters" that only seemed to eat little girls with red hair.

I swam out as far as I could go and just paddled for a moment or two, watching the people up on the beach cooking themselves or chasing their small, brightly clad children around. I was so involved in watching a woman that must have been(to my nine year old thinking) a hundred and fifty years old chasing a tiny little toddler in bright green that I got hit in the head with a beach ball. Beach balls don't hurt, but it surprised me enough to make me stop swimming and sink under, which resulted in choking and splashing and the equivalent of nine year old cussing("Stupid! Moron!") thrown every which way.

When I calmed down, I noticed that the perpetrators were watching me with big eyes, one trying not to laugh and one trying not to cry. They looked identical. Matching brown ponytails, dripping wet from

the lake, matching brown eyes, and from the straps I'd say matching green swimsuits, too. I'd never met twins before.

"Was that yours?" I asked, though I was pretty sure I knew the answer.

"Yeah, sorry. Can we have it back?" The one that talked was the one that had been trying not to laugh. She seemed braver.

"Whatever." I could tell they were "a lot" younger than me—about seven, maybe. So I had to act like the cool older girl, which wasn't something I got to do a lot. I looked around for their ball, which had either drifted, bounced, or done a neat combination of both into the lily pads. "Over there." I pointed and they looked, but they didn't move. "Aren't you going to go and get it?" They shook their heads no. I didn't need to ask why because I knew. The lily pads were scary. Everyone talked about the big fish and turtles that hid there. Having grown up around the lake, I'd seen some turtles and fish caught in the lily pads that had been HUGE (to a small-ish kid).

"Can you get it? Please?" It was the about-to-cry one that asked. Her eyes looked even bigger, and her sister copied her actions. Suddenly, I understood what my dad meant when he said someone had "puppy-dog eyes." I thought about saying no. I really,

really did. I didn't want to risk my toes in the lilies, but I also didn't want to be mean. There was a difference in being the cool, older girl and the mean, older girl. I sighed.

"Fine." We swam over to the lilies, which started near the beach and stretched past the piers, into the deep water where I never went because of the seaweed and monster stories that I still kind of believed. Thankfully, the ball was closer to the shore. We had to

walk to get even with it. The water only came up to my hips, and I tried to act very brave.

The twins wouldn't come in with me, so I had to go in all by myself. The water was warm in places, cool in others, just like everywhere else, but the bottom was different. Sharp rocks laid in ambush, covered in slick mud. It sucked at my feet, and I almost turned around because the water was getting deeper. Up to my bellybutton, then nearly to my shoulders, I finally made it to the ball. I grabbed it and made a mad dash back because I thought I'd felt fins or maybe claws on the back of my leg (it had only been a lily pad underwater). Right near the end, the

ground disappeared, and I fell into a shallow dip. When I looked down, I noticed something that made my fear disappear—a giant clam shell, bigger than both my hands and wide open. I picked it up, dumped the sand from it, and carried it in one hand and the ball under my other arm.

The twins were waiting for me with big eyes, both happy. They took the ball and then saw the shell. "Where did you get it?" they asked. I could tell they wanted one like it or the actual shell.

"The lilies. You have to be brave to get it. That's the only way." I didn't expect them to believe me, but I was still in my cool, older girl persona. They believed me, though, and the braver one walked into the lilies.

She came back out screaming about claws (again the underwater lilies) and huddled with us in the clear, shallow water. They went back off to play for several hours, and I sat on the beach, making castles for my shell. Finally, the sun dipped in the sky, and the beach emptied. The girls, who I thought had left, came up to me, soaking wet and looking at the ground.

"Can you get us a shell like yours?" Of course I couldn't. To my mind there was only one clam as big as this one, and I held it in my hands. No others existed. I debated with myself for a minute. Finally, I held it out to them.

"Here. But...bring it back tomorrow." I knew I wouldn't see them tomorrow, but they were young (younger, anyway) and nodded, took it, and left.

It was not until almost a year later that I got a package in the mailbox on a hot summer day. I opened it, wanting nothing more than to go to the beach and cool off again, but I opened it anyway. I didn't recognize the names or the address(Chicago!). In it was a letter, written by the hands of one or two eight year old girls, and under the letter, half a clam shell.

"*We never came back to the beach. Sorry. We had to go home, and it's a really long drive. But we want you to have this half. We hope it's okay to keep the other one as a reminder. Because you taught us to do things for ourselves, even though we're little and scared sometimes. But thanks.*" They had signed their names underneath, and I smiled.

I hadn't meant to teach them a life lesson, and if I had, it probably would have backfired. But I guess I taught them something, and in turn learned from it. It really opened my eyes to how what I say and do affects others. I learned that most times, the life lessons we cherish most are learned without real teachers, learned from strangers on the beach with a red pony tail, learned from lily pad monsters and even clam shells.

Who I Am

Poetry by Emily Thomas, Senior
Watercolor by Kirsten Brown, Junior

I am the back road in the summertime,
dirty feet and bright eyes finding trouble on
a log cabin farm.
Animals as my companions, I pedal into the sunset,
looking forward to a new day
I am from the strict hand with kind eyes
molding me into something respectable,
a child of God, as I stick my tongue out in Church,
such a mischievous little blonde.
I am from the paint that took me home,
An artist of music, verse and colors;
distracted by inspiration, I run to my happiness.
I am the wings of a mockingbird
trying to fit in, trying to fly.
At last I have found a flock
catching me if my wings grow weary,
my friends
I am the future, if anything.
I am the next morning, with a happy smile.
I am the beauty in diamond eyes, gazing at stars in the night sky.
I am a child, dancing to polka music, ribbons in my hair,
a sip of lemonade,
a laugh that rings.
I am yours to perceive.
I am Emily.

Peanuts and Crackerjacks

Nonfiction by Alec Carey, Senior

One of my earliest memories of my father and I comes from Wrigley Field in Chicago. It was my first Cubs game. I don't remember the details of it. I don't remember the score, the opponent, or even the date. What I do remember are the most important facts. These facts are what made it a special day for me. My father taking time off work, buying me the expensive ball park food, getting me my first baseball cap; these were the sacrifices he made. These memories I will carry with me forever.

I know it was a summer day with the sun beating down on us for hours. I remember putting on the sun tan lotion, because Mom gave Dad instructions on not letting her "baby" roast in the heat. It felt like I had another layer of skin applied to my body. We sat in the bleachers anticipating the start of the game. We watched battling practice, and Mark Grace and Sammy Sosa hit ball after ball.

Before the game began, the "Star Spangled Banner" and "Take Me Out to the Ball Game" were sung by everyone in the stands. This gave me the desire to have every food from the song I had learned to sing at a very young age. I wanted peanuts and Crackerjacks. I pleaded with my dad for the treats, and he quickly understood why. We made a trip to the concessions in-between innings so I could indulge myself in the ball park snacks. No peanuts and Crackerjacks will ever be better then the ones I at my first big league game.

Time flew by as the game progressed through the nine innings. I don't remember anything of it at all as it happened so fast! I do remember leaving the park, and walking down the long ramps of the Chicago Cub's holy ground known as Wrigley. When we exited onto the streets, my dad and I went to the vendors selling all types of merchandise. My dad got a blue hat with a large red C right in the middle, just like the players wore. This hat was for me, and I wore it the whole way home. Just before we were ready to enter the parking lot containing our car, my dad shouted to me, and we both looked on as my favorite player, Sammy Sosa, drove away in a large black SUV. I was ecstatic from that feeling of being so close to one of my heroes. When we reached the car and started home, the weariness of the day quickly took its toll on me, and I fell asleep, not waking till we arrived home.

That day meant so much to me; it made every trip to a baseball game rate not even half as exciting as that first. My dad made that day special for me. This is my first memory of a day my dad and I spent together, just father and son. It is very special to me, and not all the peanuts and Crackerjacks in the world can take that away from me.

Welcome to My Life

Poetry by Abby Johndrow, Senior
Oil by Garrett Blad, Senior
Scholastic Art Award Honorable Mention

Bright days on fresh streets.
Loud trucks roaring with food.
Stepping down onto the ground.
Apple trees blooming and leaving ammo.

Scary kids rude and friendly all alike.
Walking in green and white.
Teachers talking, words spinning.
Nervous, have no friends, what to do.

First day, what a way.
Long halls but no stairs.
Hooray!
Friends talk, others push.
Walk in, sit and wait for years.

Finally the days.
They are here which makes me cheer.
Ending will bring sweetness and sadness.
Homework thrown everywhere.
Life turning onto a highway.

Old and wrinkled but happy.
Never regretting what was never done.
Living life to all it can be.
Never a "what if" shall be spoken.
Ending will be sweet without any sorrow.

Childhood
I Hold

Throughout my life, I have had experiences that have caused me to grow up and take a more mature step in life. I have taken these steps, but unlike many others, I have not left my childhood completely behind me. I have yet to grow fully mature, and I don't feel the need to completely erase my childhood at all. I don't want to be immature, but I don't want to be a robot either. I want to stay golden, and not like those people who say they enjoyed childhood and wished they could do it all over again.

To some people, I may be mature; to others, I may be immature, but I am just me. I am grown up, but still have my little kid mentality inside. I keep it because it fills my world with wonder and happiness. Some things that kids do just make us wish we were there again, but if we try to keep our childhood as we grow, we will realize that maybe growing old isn't all that bad. If there are things that you should have done, but you think you are too old to do it, it's because you *think* like you're old. You are not aware that your childhood is still with you and that you can do it.

My friends and I all act like big kids, from bikes to just walking down the old neighborhood streets that we once were kings of, only to be handed to the next generation to run. We look back and see the scars from our bike accidents and our stupid ideas of firework wars. The reason we feel like it was just yesterday is because our childhood memories are telling us what fun it is to be young and that we should never let go of it. I take that as a sign that I better take every chance I can to be the kid that I really am, the one who is still

Nonfiction by Mark Davis, Senior

Charcoal by Amanda Bachtel, Senior
Scholastic Art Award Honorable Mention

inside me.

If people tell you to "grow up," perhaps they're just in denial of their childhood. Society pushes each of us to be a robot and have a serious face once we mysteriously "grow up." The way I see it, if you can be told to grow up and act your age *and still* hold on to your inner child, you are more free than any others in the world because you didn't let society get a grip on you and pull you down into the hole of conformism. Make all you can of your adult life, but also enjoy it by keeping your childhood and making it a valuable part of you.

I'll probably never get rid of my childishness, and I never plan on it. I'm going to stay this way, and I'm not going to let anything change it. It's the most valuable treasure. Enjoy it. Don't ever let it go, and don't ever let someone else strip it from you. I never regret "being a kid," and I'll never regret growing up now either.

Sue, the Dinosaur, Chews BUBBLEGUM

*Fiction
by Ben Weiss,
Sophomore*

*Pencil
by Cheyenne McLachlan,
Senior*

Four years ago my family went down to Florida for the first part of Christmas Break. The plan was to leave school two days in advance, spend a week checking out the Everglades, DisneyWorld, go to the beach, you know, just your usual Florida vacation. Then, fly back the morning of Christmas Eve and be back for Christmas at Grandma's. Sounds like a dream come true, right? Sunny days in the middle of December, then spend the morning on a quick flight to South Bend to be home for a white Christmas. It didn't work out that way.

The first part of break was great. We went to Disney, checked out Miami, saw the sights and what not. The problem occurred when we were packing our bags for the flight home. Apparently, someone misplaced the airplane tickets. We searched high and low for our tickets, but they were nowhere to be found. Dad was the one who finally called it quits.

"Well, guys, we have to leave, or the hotel is going to charge us for another day." I think Sam, my second youngest brother, and I were both glad to finally be done looking, and we bolted out the door and down to the lobby. Gabe, my youngest brother, was four and didn't pay much attention. He just played with some little paper snakes he learned to make in preschool art class. Mom and Dad, I suppose, were not quite ready to accept the unexpected hole that was just burned in their wallet, and dragged their feet on the way out, each taking one last look around.

"I guess we're going to have to go to the airport," Dad sighed, "to see if we can't get something worked out."

The line at the airport help desk was mind-boggling. When we got there, we all stared in disbelief. Then, slowly, all four of our heads turned toward the back of the line. The line snaked through rows of stanchions down along the wall, past a Salvation Army Santa, all the way down to a giant floor-to-ceiling window decorated with flashing green and red lights, and then turned down a hallway to who knows where.

Well, I can tell you where. We trudged to the back of the line, past drumming fingers and tapping feet. We could feel a thousand suspicious eyes on us. Eyes of people who had spent the better part of the morning fending off line-cutters and listening to the maddening Christmas carols replayed over the loudspeaker. At the back of the line, we were stuck behind a far eastern Indian family. Gabe looked up from his snakes to peer at them. His brow wrinkled up on his baby-face.

"Why are those people wearing red stickers on their foreheads?" he asked.

Sam and I both busted up,

but dutifully tried to pinch our lips together as tightly as we could and breathe smoothly. "Shh!" whispered Mom and Dad. "Those aren't stickers. Don't talk about it right now."

"They aren't?" he asked. "Well, then what are they?" he said, not making any particular effort to keep his voice lowered.

"Shh!" they whispered again. "We will talk about it later," putting an end to it with the looks on their faces. They turned back to their own conversation, and Gabe returned to his family of snakes. Sam and I looked at each other and smothered our laughs.

A little while later, I suppose we were being too rowdy and the line wasn't budging, so our parents turned to us and gave us the run-through. Dad was going to stay here and wait in line, and we were going to go to lunch and find something to do for an hour or so. We parted ways and headed to the food court. We each got our own large pretzel, bag of chips, and a lemonade, a special treat. Gabe didn't want to finish his. He wanted to get back to playing with his snakes on the floor. Sam and I polished his off. We returned to Dad in the line and were glad to see he had made at least two feet of progress.

After a long day of waiting in line, trips to the food court and bathrooms, we finally got to the front of the line. I don't really remember what was said. "Grown-up talk" was boring, and Sam and I were too absorbed in counting the number of sleeping people we could see. Regardless, it took forever, and we moved on to count all the people running. When they were finally done, Dad looked angry, and Mom looked exhausted. They put on their "We're going to have an adventure" faces and told Sam and I that we were going to need to hurry to catch a different flight. Translation: We needed to run. Sam and I giggled at this. Mom picked up

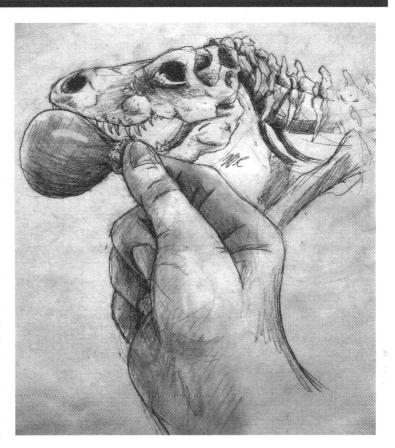

Gabe, who was still playing with those paper snakes, to carry him. Then, we were off.

We barely made it on time. The three of us boys sat next to each other. Gabe wanted the window seat. It was only his second flight, so he wanted to stare out the window the whole time. After that, came me, and Sam by the aisle. Mom and Dad sat in front of us. The flight was pretty uneventful. I fell asleep, but woke up when we encountered some pretty bad turbulence near O'Hare International.

After we landed, the plan was to catch a plane over to South Bend that was due to leave at five o'clock. However, when five o'clock rolled around and we were in our seats on the plane, the control tower wouldn't give us the okay to leave. The delay was due to a severe snowstorm raging all across the Midwest. We sat on the tarmac for hours. We even taxied onto

the runway twice, but both times we had to turn back. Finally, they let us back off the plane and into the terminal because our cause was growing more and more futile as the night wore on.

We were all exhausted by then and just wanted to lie down. All except for Gabe. Gabe had heard about Sue the dinosaur and really wanted to see her. Too tired to argue, we lugged our bags over to the ancient reptile's skeleton. To Gabe it was enlightening. To the rest of us, it just meant we got to lie down. Gabe dumped his suitcase and ran over to jump around her ankles or something while the rest of us collapsed against the nearest wall.

Three hours later, we were all sitting against the wall, completely numb, bored out of our minds. All of us, that is, except Gabe, who was playing with his paper snakes again. He seemed to be unaware of time passing. Lucky kid. I hadn't really ever looked at his little snake things. He had eleven of them. Ten were gray and blue; the other one was green and looked like construction paper. They looked like strips of paper that were folded back and forth, so that the final product was stringy and had a smiley face drawn on the end square. Gabe paused and looked up at me. I asked him if I could play. He nodded and handed me one of the gray and blue ones.

"You can be this one," he said. "This is my guy. His name is Fang," indicating the green one. I studied my snake and realized right away that it was half of one of our original plane tickets!

"Gabe!" I exclaimed. "What is this?"

"A snake," he said, with a look that called me stupid.

"Mom, Dad, look. Gabe's snakes are our plane tickets!"

"What?" everyone asked in disbelief.

"Look." I passed one to everyone so they could see the proof.

Gabe was already in a defensive pout, even though he wasn't quite sure what he had done wrong.

Well, that put everyone in a bad mood. Mom and Dad half-heartedly chewed Gabe out about "taking Mommy and Daddy's things," but they gave it up pretty quickly.

Outside, the situation was getting more and more hopeless. They came on the speaker system and gave the bad news: "Due to severe snowstorms, all commercial air traffic has been restricted at this time. The traffic restriction will be in effect at least until two a.m. We will let you know when we have any more news. We apologize for the inconvenience and . . . have a Merry Christmas."

This was obviously terrible news, and the mood of the airport plummeted from anxious and nervous to deflated and hopeless. We all slumped further down against our suitcases. I looked around for the thousandth time, and for the thousandth time, my eyes caught on the Sue Souvenir Shop. I stared at it, not because it was anything special, but it was just the only interesting thing in the whole place. My stomach growled and told me I was hungry again. I was always hungry these days. I wondered if they had anything to eat in there. Probably not. It didn't look like it sold any food, but maybe they had candy bars... or gum! Gum would keep my stomach quiet, I reasoned. Gum was invented for hungry, teenaged boys because of food shortages during

> **I realize this isn't very funny to anyone who wasn't there, but to us, given our situation and current state of mind, the ludicrous notion of the bubble coming out of the dinosaur's mouth was appropriate**

World War I. Or was it? My stomach growled again.

"Mom," I asked, "can I go see if that souvenir shop has any gum?"

"Sure."

"Can I have a dollar?"

She gave it to me. I stood up, readjusted my shirt, and headed to the shop. As it turned out, they did sell gum. Extra Ice Mint, Stride Tropical Blast, and my favorite, that Hubba Bubba stuff that has the goose with all the piercings in its beak. I bought the Hubba Bubba, and popped a piece in my mouth on the way back across the giant room. I sat back down and dealt out a piece to everyone.

I watched Gabe unwrap his piece and pop it into his mouth. He laced his fingers together behind his head while leaning back as he started to chew, and immediately, he started blowing bubbles. He had just learned the ancient art of bubble blowing and was very proud to be able to exhibit his technique. It was the first time all day I could remember that I had seen him do anything by choice that didn't involve his snakes. He sighed and looked up at Sue who was grinning a giant grin down on top of us. Gabe blew an impressive bubble. He glanced down his nose at it and plucked it out to admire it. It was about the size of a softball. He studied it from a few different angles. Then he looked back up at Sue and back down at his gum. He grinned. He held the bubble out at arm's length towards Sue's mouth and laughed. We all turned to look at him.

"Imagine if Sue were able to chew bubble gum," he giggled.

I realize this isn't very funny to anyone who wasn't there, but to us, given our situation and current state of mind, the ludicrous notion of the bubble coming out of the dinosaur's mouth was appropriate for us finally accepting that Christmas this year wasn't going to be what we had hoped for.

We started out with just a few chuckles, then a few ha-ha's, and finally, we couldn't hold it in. It felt good to laugh, so we didn't hold back. It made us let go of all that had happened that day and just relax and find some humor in our unfortunate situation.

The next morning, we boarded a plane at eleven o'clock. Gabe brought with him a Sue notepad Mom bought him as an early Christmas present. There were still a few flakes straggling behind, lazily winding their way down to the ground as we touched down in South Bend. We got home at around 12:30. We were late to Grandma's house, but everyone was glad we made it. And, as luck would have it, Gabe got a set of rubber snakes in the white elephant gift exchange.

Holding On To Memories

Nonfiction by Kirsten Brown, Junior

The majority of my childhood memories are nothing more than blurred images lost among the debris in the jungle of my mind, seemingly no more important than anything happening to any stranger halfway around the world. I was a different person in the past. When I think back to when I was younger, it seems as if I am reading someone else's autobiography-an autobiography with extraordinary imagery and amazing detail. Although this leaves plenty of energy to direct towards the future, sometimes I'm sad that I can't remember more of my past. So much time is spent regretting the past that I have no room left to store the good memories. I believe that I often miss out on beautiful moments because I only keep room for the best and the worst memories. But the past is a mysterious thing. I often remember random memories when I least expect it. Something as simple as a television commercial or magazine cover can awaken dormant images in my mind.

Perhaps another reason I can never recall my younger years is because they were so dreadfully boring. My parents' protection was purely out of love. Unfortunately, their love made for some memories that weren't lovely. I can remember more times being bored than anything else. But my boredom eventually led to creativity and imagination. Maybe I owe them after all. By draining a bit of fun out of my childhood, they increased my skills in my teen years. Still, I have to wonder if I wouldn't have been just as creative if I would have been allowed to do what other kids did. I believe I could have had my cake and still be eating it for a very long time.

The past may be hard for me to grasp, but there are a few memories that still seem as real as the second they happened. One of these memories, one of my favorites, consists of nothing more than a sofa and a ton of stuffed friends. I'm not sure why this day sticks out in my mind. I can remember every second. The sofa was a house, a school bus, and a park, all in one day. I remember waking up before my parents, which almost never happened. I spent the entire day playing make believe in my room. I remember the ugly floral wallpaper that used to hang on the walls and the shadows of my window frames across my wooden floor. It was a truly enchanting moment, one that I never want to forget.

Sadly, memory isn't something we can control. I learned this watching my grandfather's memory slowly dissipate until it vanished altogether. Memory isn't permanent. I'm just hoping that someday, by the time I'm my grandfather's age, some doctor somewhere will find a miraculous pill to keep my favorite memories right where I want them. If I'm too old to look forward to the future, I want to be able to at least look back to the past.

Rockin' with a Banjo

Nonfiction by Mariah Rippy, Junior
Watercolor by Mariah Rippy, Junior
Scholastic Art Award Silver Key

When I was little, storms used to frighten me. I'm not exactly sure when it started, but one night my father coaxed me out to the front porch with him during a rather mild conflict in the sky. I was scared at first, not only by the loud crashes, but the bright flashes of light showing the outlines of the clouds. We were safe from the rain, the roof of our house jutting out above to protect the porch. Now and then the wind would blow the rain in our direction, and we'd get small sprays of water in our faces, but it wasn't troublesome.

My father moved to sit on an old rocking chair, one we still have to this day, and I hurried to sit on his lap. He had his leather banjo case with him. It probably wasn't leather, though the texture always reminded me of the smooth fabric. He moved around me to pull his banjo out, and afterwards rested it on both of our laps, his hands settling on the strings, a metal finger pick already on his thumb and index finger. I always saw the finger picks as claws, and tried my best to avoid touching them, though it amazed me how helpful they were to my father when he began to strum rapid notes. He'd do a few warm ups, but eventually the warm ups would flow into structured songs. His medley would consist of "Twinkle Twinkle Little Star," a version that one could hardly tell was the simple child's lullaby. "You Are My Sunshine," and older folk songs I didn't particularly recognize as my young self.

"You Are My Sunshine" was the only song he sang the words to, and it was an immediate comfort during nature's quarrel. As ironic as it may seem, I'd hear the song as background music for the lightning show, and it would make me feel like the most privileged child in the universe to have my dad singing it to me. I'd always imagined that he had written it, the first verse at least, just for his little daughter, to sing to her when she was scared or worried about something. He probably sang the tune to me before the moments on the porch, but before then I never appreciated it as much. As I recall, he continued singing it to me thereafter, and now and then I can catch him humming or singing along to it on the radio. Presently, I have to practically beg him to get his banjo out because he claims that he hasn't played it in ages. I always hope that his fingers will remember the melody and strums of "You Are My Sunshine," just so I can have the constant remembrance to when I was a child.

COMING TO America

Nonfiction by Ben Keller, Senior

The story of the Lenz family has been passed down from my great-grandmother to my mother. It is known that my great-grandmother, Helena Rose Heymig, came to the United States from Nazi Germany in 1937 with her father and mother, her sister Ann her other sister, Mary, and her brother Henry. This much of the story is fact. From there, the stories start forming from many people in my family. The story that I was first told goes a little like this.

My great great-grandfather, Heinrich, was living in Nuremberg with my great great-grandmother, Ziegfreida and their three children. Heinrich had fought in World War I and was almost killed during a battle in France. He realized how horrible of a state Germany was in, and he knew what was best for his family. The only thing he could think to do was to come to America. So he and Ziegfreida started saving up money so they could buy land in the United States. Their plans were halted by the rise of the fascist dictator Adolph Hitler. Heinrich knew that the time had come, whether they were ready or not. The plan was to send Grandpa Heinrich's brother, Emmerich, to America to buy land for the Heymig's to live on. Emmerich went to Naples, Italy, to go on a boat to the United States, but Emmerich's greed got a hold of him. He took the money he was given, and gambled all of it away. By the time this news got to Grandma and Grandpa Heymig, Hitler had become chancellor, and their lives were in danger. Heinrich knew he had to at least get out of Germany even if they couldn't get out of Europe. So the whole family packed up and left Nuremberg and made the long trek to the small town of Fiox in France. They lived there for three months until Hitler invaded France. Even though they were not ready, the time had come, nonetheless. Heinrich, Ziegfreida, Ann, Mary, and Henry were smuggled onto a boat that was headed to Ellis Island.

The boat trip there took about two weeks during which my great-grandmother, Oma, turned 7. Before she passed, my Oma told us about the ride over. She said that the boat was like a skater slipping across the icy sea. She only told my grandmother about the family's story before she passed. This is what my grandmother put together from the stories Oma told her.

When Oma got here, the Heymigs went through Ellis Island and headed for the steel metropolis of Gary, Inidana. When they arrived in the ""New World," it was like a 10,000 lb weight had been lifted off their chest. Heinrich the worked in the mills, helping the United States win the war. Oma told us that while they still lived in Gary, her Aunt Frieda, Heinrich's sister, mailed him a letter telling him that Emmerich had gone back to Nuremberg, and had died in the Battle of Stalingrad. She told us that Grandpa Heinrich burned the letter after he read it and never spoke of anyone in our family who still lived in Germany. After the war, Grandpa Heinrich and Grandma Ziegfreida bought a farm in the small Indiana town of Walkerton, Indiana. My great great-grandmother and grandfather both passed, and my Oma took over the farm with her husband, Roger Lenz. Roger and Oma had seven children together: my grandmother, Jean Ann; my great-aunts, Helene, Bernadette, Theresa, Brenda and Judy; and my uncle David. Sadly after battling with lung cancer, Roger passed away, leaving my Oma a widow with seven children. Oma stayed strong as she grew older, and my great aunts and uncle grew older and started having children of their own.

My family has many different variations of stories that were passed on by Oma, Ann, Mary, and Henry. Their first-hand accounts haven't been written down until now. Today, only Mary, the baby, survives. My Oma passed her story down to her children, and they passed it down to their children, and they passed it down to my siblings and me. They had only one chance, one hope, one dream. The story of the Heymig family is an epic story, and I'm proud to tell it.

Heart of an Artist

Nonfiction by Mariah Rippy, Junior

Oil by Garrett Blad, Senior
Scholastic Art Award Silver Key

Excitement used to grow within me as my class lined up at the door to make our way to the art room in elementary school. I'd feel a sudden happiness, and realize that where I was about to go was an escape from the dull, monotonous lessons we'd get in history, math, or reading. I would always look forward to what our art teacher, Mrs. Setnor, had in store for us to do.

Sometimes she'd give us a lesson on an artist like Picasso or Van Gogh. We'd draw an image relative to what they painted- our own bedroom, for example, or what we saw outside our window. We'd draw distorted faces and then we'd work on clay to mimic the sculptors we were educated on. Whatever I finished, I'd take home to my parents so they could hang the silly, inexperienced work of art on the fridge or store it in a crate for safe keeping. When we looked back on it many years later, we'd laugh at the sweet artifacts of childhood.

I've always enjoyed art. Whether drawing, painting, scratching, or sculpting, the feeling simply grew within me right along with the physical growth of my body. In elementary school I saw it as something fun to do, a hobby, really. As I grew older, I emerged from the immaturity and ignorance of primary school. Art not only became more fun, but it became more serious to me. It was something I knew I wanted to do for the rest of my life.

In middle school I worked harder at becoming better at what I did. I always imagined it to be the beginning of the seriousness of becoming an adult. Seventh grade to me was more important than being a freshman, then. I'd have to be one of the better art students in my class in order to secure a spot for myself in the art career pool after high school.

Having thought of art as fun in elementary school really helps me out to this day, because when I look back to the simplicity of primary art, I remember that art can be both serious and enjoyable. It has to be enjoyable for me to be able to make something out of it. What is painting without feeling? What is a sculpture without emotion intertwined with every cut of the fettling knife or every hit of the chisel? Art is nothing without human emotion. There is no point to it if there is not feeling or thought involved. Yet seriousness is a key ingredient to successfully putting together a beautiful masterpiece, as well. One must be serious when organizing the creativity and layout of a certain piece, in order for it to be taken seriously by others.

Every moment of experience I've had with art- whether it's when I was a child drawing on the back of place mat at a restaurant, or now, working up a portfolio for college- counts. Everything is added together in the end, like grains of sand worked into stone to form a sure and precise figure that people will remember for who knows how long. My thoughts of art being my life are just as strong, if not stronger, then they were in middle school. Except now, I can actually make things happen.

CANVAS

Poetry by Ayla Felix, Senior
Oil by Catrina Kroeger, Senior

A blank canvas, stark and white, though not really white
because white implies that something is already there
to show the difference, but nothing is; it's just empty.
A pencil, long and solid and real. And suddenly the nothing is just white
because there is a harsh dark line marring it, giving it life, a life as of yet undefined.
A few more pencil strokes and suddenly it's an image, a picture of life
captured and held still forever and for eternity. A moment in time, never changing.
A palette, paints. Brushes. Simple and abstract, they mean nothing apart,
but everything when they are used together.
The first, tentative stroke, testing the color, the brush, the hand. Suddenly, the canvas
really is white because the line is not.
More colors. Peach, orange, blue, maroon. Just colors, clumsy shapes barely making sense
on the canvas, which is no longer white because it's color.
Lines, definitive and there, over the pencil, over the color. And suddenly the nothing
which had undefined life is given definition.
The soft curve of a cheek, the sharp lines of a nose, the gentle contours of two pink lips.
Highlights, shadows. Blending.
The face on the canvas stares up at me, and I find myself on the canvas mirror
smiling ever so slightly, thankful that I've chosen me
for this little bit of captured eternity.

MIRROR

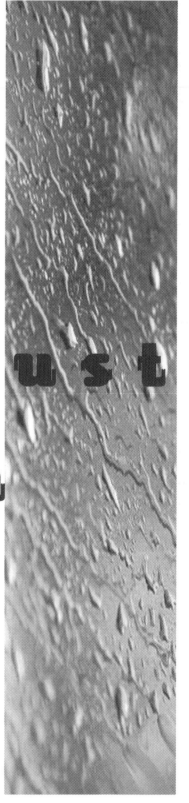

As I watched out the window, music filled the car. I was moving down the road to a place I'd been many times before. For some reason, this would be the time that stayed in my head. It was different than all the times before. This time, it was raining.

I was traveling to Borders. I always love going to Borders or any bookstore. We weren't going for any special reason. There were no last minute presents I had to buy, and there was no money in my pocket to burn. Nonetheless, we were on our way.

Looking back, I think the

Nonfiction by Nick Havranek,
Junior
Acrylic by Emily Thomas, Senior

It's Just
Rain

reason I specifically remember this trip was because it was raining. I watched the rain slide down the windows like little snakes that would race each other to the bottom. The smell in the air was intoxicating. That is another reason I can recall this memory so vividly. I can remember smelling that distinct aroma. It was like a mixture of roses and an ocean. I couldn't want more than that.

Rain always seems to play a significant role in my memories. It just seems pure and calming. Rain is like this terrible force that can take away everything and leave you with nothing or it can help you see things you could never see before.

Another time rain was in a somewhat special memory was my first "real" girlfriend. I don't really know if it was just another middle school, love-desperation relationship, but regardless, she was my first kiss. I remember just sitting in her room talking and watching the rain outside. The lightning would strike and light up a silhouette of the trees in the distance. It was beautiful. We just sat in her room for hours. The rain was a calming factor in this memory, and I don't think I could remember it as well without the rain. It probably would have been another boring, pointless night without the rain.

That girl was my first kiss, but, if I could, I'd take it back in a heartbeat. This memory has more of a bittersweet sadness for me than anything else. The rain was a memento of both my first kiss and my first lost love.

Thinking back, I can recall another time rain was very crucial to my memory. Mariah, Robby, and I were all hanging out at Robby's house. We were playing video games and watching videos on the internet just like every other teenager alive today, when, suddenly, the power went out. It was around nine at night, so it was pretty dark in the house. We had to find candles and flashlights to use. But then we got an idea. We could tell scary stories! We also got the idea to build a fort out of sheets and blankets and tell scary stories under that. It was like we were ten again. I know it might sound silly, but I don't think anything could be better than just making a fort with your friends. It's always a bonding

the walls that the world has built around you and you're deciding to put

up your own. You're making up your own rules, and everyone else has to follow them. It's your world.

The rain in that story was a happy, destructive force. It also brought us all closer together, and I don't think that night would've been nearly as amazing without the rain. Even though we didn't have the internet or TV to entertain us, we had each other. I don't think that anything else could've been quite as memorable.

Another memory I have surrounding rain is the day that I was at Kirsten's house. We were eating, and all of a sudden we saw lightning, and it started raining. I looked out the window, and I could see the gigantic, rolling, greenish-gray clouds heading straight towards the house.

Her dad made us go downstairs and watch the TV for any news on the storm. It was a bad one. The storm had taken down some power lines and lasted for at least an

hour. I was actually frightened by that thought. Even though an hour doesn't seem like that long of a time period, it seemed like an eternity when I was scared.

All through this storm, I was texting my mom and letting her know that I wasn't dead. She would make a joke, and I would make a joke, and I'd feel so much safer. So I sat on the couch and watched the fading picture on the television for any signs of the storm letting up.

Then, it was over. The rain just stopped. As the thunder reverberated in the background, I texted my dad to let him know that the storm had passed us and he could safely come to pick me up. We all went upstairs and sat in the kitchen for awhile until my dad finally arrived.

The rain in this story seemed to only be a kind of evil force. It was simply there to harm. I couldn't see anything good coming out of this storm in anyway. But now I think that this was a bonding experience more for my mom and I in a way. Even though I was with Kirsten and her family, I felt like I was at home.

Rain has affected me in more ways than I thought possible. One might think that it's just rain, but, to me, it's a sign that I can move on. It's a sign that I can grow stronger. The rain is a sign that I can be me and not be afraid of the walls caving in.

Plato at McDonald's

Poetry by Kelsey Piotrowicz, Senior

The old Ford pick-up putters its way to his usual parking spot.
With wise wrinkles and forgotten eyes, he steps out into the morning.
Golden arches illuminate the 5 a.m. sky.
As he opens the door, a warm hazelnut aroma smacks his senses.
"Welcome to McDonald's. How can I help you?" asks the forget-me-not woman behind the counter
      in her cigarette enhanced voice.
"A medium coffee, please, with a shot of vanilla," requests Old Plato.
As he waits, the stack of morning papers catches his eye.
"Oh, the public," he thinks aloud as he shakes his head at the horrifying headlines.
Coffee in hand, he walks to his usual table, the familiar layer of grime smooth
      to the touch of his morose fingers.
Throughout the morning, people stare at the lonely old man at the corner table.
His straggly beard and shaggy hair only contradict the respectable robes that hang from his shoulders.
But he is watching them, too.
Ethically, mathematically, physically, philosophically, he sits pondering people
      and society in the dining room of a McDonald's.
He spies on the old men discussing the government and telling dirty jokes,
      the father and son getting breakfast before their annual fishing trip,
      the five girls who have been up all night who enter with matching pajamas and laughter.
These are the people of life.
He doesn't speak to anyone, only a nod or a smile.
Then a brave little girl in a pink princess dress and cowboy boots walks up and
      taps him on the shoulder.
    "Are you a king?"
    "Yes, a philosopher king."
    "Well, I'm a princess. I need help with something, though. I have a question for you."
    "And what's that, princess?"
    "McNuggets or a cheeseburger? What are you going to eat?"
He smiles, like the Ronald McDonald statue next to him, and says,
    "Even a Platonic guardian couldn't tell you that.
     But as I once told Socrates, dear, *knowledge* is the food of the soul."

Monkey Jim

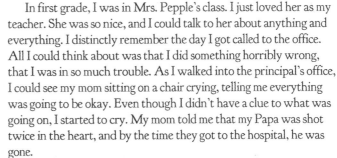

Nonfiction by Micki Dennie, Senior
Photo of Monkey Jim by Micki Dennie, Senior

I have a stuffed animal that I got in the first grade. I remember the exact day I got it. It was so fluffy and soft. When you looked at it, you just had to smile. That's what it is there for, to make you smile. You are probably wondering why I am talking about a stupid stuffed animal, what does it have to do with a memory? It deals with every memory I have of my Papa Didier. Every time I look at that purple monkey with hearts around its neck, all I think about is that dreadful first grade year.

In first grade, I was in Mrs. Pepple's class. I just loved her as my teacher. She was so nice, and I could talk to her about anything and everything. I distinctly remember the day I got called to the office. All I could think about was that I did something horribly wrong, that I was in so much trouble. As I walked into the principal's office, I could see my mom sitting on a chair crying, telling me everything was going to be okay. Even though I didn't have a clue to what was going on, I started to cry. My mom told me that my Papa was shot twice in the heart, and by the time they got to the hospital, he was gone.

I remember having to go home to pack so I could go to my dad's house for Papa's funeral. I remember his wrinkly face all full of life. It was always so red with laughter. Then I had to see him lying so peacefully in the casket, his face pale and lifeless. It was so hard to see him like that. After the funeral I faintly remember going back to my dad's house. All I can remember is seeing the man's face that killed him on the news. A 17 year old. Did he know what he was doing? Did he know that he was taking the life of a man so loving, so kind to everyone, a man that every time he saw me, told me how much he loved my freckles and how that's one of the reason's he married my Nana. It made me feel so special when he told me that. It's been eleven years now. The time has flown by. It's so crazy to think about it.

When I came back to school the following week, my teacher gave me that stuffed animal: a purple monkey with hearts around its neck. When you look at it straight on, you can't even see the eyes. All you can see is the gigantic smile. It makes me happy just looking at it, and helps me forget the bad year. I named that stuffed animal Monkey Jim after my Papa. It's just perfect, isn't it?

In Tune with Oneself

Fiction by J. J. Silvey, Sophomore
Pencil by Mackenzie Hill, Junior

It was quiet as the sun set. The opaque, soft shades of orange, purple, and red blended subtly into an enigmatic phenomenon. All of this beauty took place right outside of the window of Julian Reid, yet she never paused to part the curtains and take in the simplistic beauty of the sunset. Instead, she spent her time on the inside of her Manhattan apartment. Julian sat there, on the edge of her bead, playing her violin. The dark yet soft tone reverberated off her walls and sung a melancholy tune, almost perfectly in time with the unified beat of the metropolis that surrounded her. Julian practiced and practiced, lost in her world of melodies and tone colors. The soft ripple of her fingers created an intense vibrating timbre, every note pouring out as an extension of her soul, but it wasn't good enough. Julian knew that it took more than passion and discipline to get into Juilliard. To the outside observer, Julian was a seventeen-year-old of prodigious skill, but in her opinion, she had much more room to grow. No matter how well she played a piece, no matter how flawless her technique, she was never be satisfied.

Some called her a perfectionist; others praised her determination, but it never went to

her head. She just continued to practice. Of course, she had passion, but no matter how much she improved, she never paused, never stopped to breathe in the fruits of her hours of practice. It was not until the night before her audition that she discovered the error of her ways. The sun was setting in its usual manner, and just before Julian shut her blinds, she observed the faint colors melting together and was moved.

The colors grew more intense as they neared the horizon, and the light refracted off of her pale-green eyes. She immediately grabbed her violin and dashed outside the apartment. Her parents were dazed by her actions. Just as the final traces of light graced the horizon, Julian's violin uttered one placid note, and the day was gone. She continued to play, with the night as her conductor. The city was her symphony, and she, its featured soloist. Her calm, placid notes erupted into a wildly improvised cadenza from her soul. The chills of the electric air sent shocks up her arms. She closed her eyes and continued the ballad. The notes immersed her in a pool of life and color. The sounds emitted from this violin, neigh, this *Stradivarius*, were a euphonic testament to life and nature. And so, Julian Reid stood there, feeling the music pulse through her. It was her life's blood, her passion. No one could take this away from her. When she retracted her bow from the violin and her private symphony cease, she opened her eyes. She had an audience. Hundreds of onlookers cheered and praised her. Roses were thrown, and many a man was brought to tears. Julian, always humble, bowed and returned home.

She never spoke of that night. She didn't have to. The pale green of her eyes gave way to a dazzling emerald shade, just as the peace and opaqueness of the sunset gives way to a clear and bright night. Julian Reid went to sleep that night with the curtains open, the moon shining on her face. Tomorrow was a day of reckoning, but she knew...it was finally good enough.

Indonesia's Freedom

Poetry by Ardy Kusuma and Priyanka Nurkhalida,
Junior, Indonesian Exchange Student
Pencil by Priyanka Nurkhalida, Junior

said something about this country
said something you never see
don't look down on us, or even on me
you don't know what this nation can be

won't let you take Indonesia
we never give our fatherland
because here, destiny lays in God's hand
with gift from our heroes, our greatest men

it isn't as superior as America
but here lies the beauty of Asia
the ocean across Pacific and Indian
the nation of freedom, Indonesia

freedom to hear, freedom to speak
freedom to express, freedom to confess
freedom of tolerance, freedom of democracy
freedom to be you, freedom to be me

there are so many races and religions
but we still have one blood in common
that's why difference is our union
dignity I put in this nation

Deeper Water

Nonfiction by Kirsten Brown, Junior

Photo of Kirsten Brown's Grandfather

We sit on the edge of my rickety pier, the sunset reflecting into my eyes. Tiny fish flicker in and out of sight, making a maze of the verdant seaweed that dances below our toes. The cool breeze makes the water feel warmer than the air. This is an all too familiar scene. We're sitting close together and not saying a word. It's comfortable. There are a million different things being said through our silence. The waves gently roll onto the beach, causing the sand to darken for a moment, only to return to its original color in the blink of an eye. I recall how strong these waves seemed to be when I was younger. No matter how hard I fought, I was always pushed back towards the shore. Now that I'm older and not as weak, it's easy to walk into the deeper water. I can handle the force.

The beautiful parts of life happen when you least expect them. It's the little things that make the difference. I can still see my living room on Christmas morning. I was either 6 or 7 years old. I had worn myself out trying to figure out what was in that bright red box. That silver bow had been a temptation for weeks, and now was the day I would finally find out what mystery it was holding back from me. I remember waking up many times during the night and eagerly checking the red glow of the alarm clock next to my bed. When I finally woke up at a reasonable time, I jumped out of bed and sprinted down the stairs. After a painfully slow breakfast and equally dreadful wait for my grandparents to arrive, it was finally time to discover the mystery. With a deep breath, I set my hands to work as quickly as I could. When I shredded the paper covering that shiny new radio, I felt like I had solved the mystery of the Holy Grail. It's too bad things like that aren't my biggest worries anymore. I was young, and things were a lot simpler, but I never really reached the deeper water in my life.

The sun is gone now, but there's still warmth in the air. We'll probably go inside pretty soon. My worst fear is that the conversation will stop if we change our surroundings. The best conversations always seem to be unplanned. Talking is best at 4 am, when you can barely make sense, but every word seems to mean so much more. Feelings come out and honesty remains. I remember every second of an early morning dialogue I shared with my best friend. We were suppose to be asleep, but we had far too many subjects to cover that night. It was a simple, beautiful thing. There was nothing romantic or dramatic about it. It was just person to person. It was probably one of the happiest moments in my memory, and I'll always remember that night. We were both exhausted and the sofa cushions were far too inviting to resist, but somehow we managed to stay awake. Maybe it was because we were both in the mood to vent and discuss current challenges. Maybe we just needed to catch up on some things we missed in each other's lives. It was at this point that I realized I had found the deeper water and was drowning in it. I struggled for quite some time. It was nearly impossible to keep my head above the surface, let alone move forward.

Another memory that constantly stays with me is a vision of my grandfather. Unfortunately, it's not a happy vision. I can only picture him the last time I saw him alive. He was frail. An old, worn blanket was folded across his lap. A nurse pushed him down the hall at the nursing home. He couldn't move his own wheelchair anymore. A vacant expression covered his face for the last few years of his life. As he drew near us, nothing on his face changed. He didn't recognize us at all. Whenever I think about my grandfather, I remember how fragile life is. It's terrifying to think of life getting so overwhelming that it can't be controlled. I know his condition had nothing to do with circumstances in his life, but it still makes me wonder how much a person can take before it's too much to handle. How deep can the water get before you're completely out of air?

Luckily, things have calmed down a lot

lately. Certain aspects of my life are much clearer than they've ever been. The older I get, the easier it is to fight through the waves of life. Is it because I'm stronger, or is it because I have friends that help me battle through? Either way, I reach deeper and deeper water everyday.

The (Not So) Good 'Ole Days

Nonfiction by Sean Heckman-Davis, Senior

Colored Pencil by Mariah Rippy, Junior

Scholastic Art Award Silver Key

I don't think my childhood ever died. I can't recall any particular moment when I suddenly stopped being a child. For me, it was really more of a gradual slide into maturity rather than an abrupt jolt; and even now I indulge in occasional fits of whimsy. Do I despair the loss of my childhood? I can't say I do. I much more enjoy being a young adult than being a child.

It seems to be human nature to desire and glorify things we cannot have or things that we have lost. I've come to this conclusion through both observation and personal experience. During the dog days of August, I lust for the cold, quiet nights of winter. And during the wet, frigid month of January, I catch myself wishing for summer. Glorification of childhood is similar to this. People seem to remember only the good memories of childhood, glossing over the bad experiences.

Childhood isn't all Holden Caulfield, the main character in the novel Catcher in the Rye, makes it out to be. When I was a kid, I had no control over my own life. I ate what my parents wanted me to eat, and slept at what they deemed reasonable hours. I went where they wanted me to go, and did what they wanted me to do. No one took me seriously, and when I was in trouble, I was expected to ask an adult for assistance.

Childhood wasn't all fun and games either. Bullying and teasing ran rampant in the playgrounds of my youth, and I took part in them. Anyone who thinks children are innocent is misremembering. As novelist Terry Pratchet wrote, "There is nothing as sweet as the sounds of children playing, provided you are too far away to actually make out what they're saying." Children can be downright cruel. I'm sure I wasn't the only one to step on ants as a kid, or cut up worms with plastic shovels, or trap toads under buckets on asphalt on a hot day waiting for them to cook. People tend to look past childhood's wanton violence and make excuses for its actions, but I certainly knew exactly what I was doing.

I think people are simply nostalgic for the times when they didn't have to do much, where nothing was expected of them, and they could sleep in the middle of the day. As I stated before, I don't share these feelings. It was a personal epiphany when I realized I didn't have to be a child to be lazy.

The Spark of Youth

Poetry Renga by Emily Thomas, Senior;
Danielle Wroblewski, Senior; Christina Newhart, Senior;
Cody Phillips, Junior; and Mariah Rippy, Junior
Charcoal by Samantha Palmer, Junior

It was night, with the
humid wind almost blowing my
sparkler out. I spell my name.

Little silver flames fly off, landing
like a safe reminder of a gentle
kiss of heat against my skin.

Flames dancing in the breeze, throwing
more wood on the fire and watching the
sparks fly in the dark night sky.

The smell of sulfur
stinging my nostrils,
yet it's almost a pleasant feeling.

I light another sparkler and rewrite
my name.
I am youth.

What If

Nonfiction by Miranda Kafantaris,
Junior
Charcoal by Ayla Felix, Senior

What if. Two hopeless words that I never want to find myself pondering on my death bed. What if I had told him how I felt when we were running through the parking lot in the rain together that one Thursday night? What if I had dreamed bigger? What if I'd made fewer excuses for my stupid mistakes? What if I had stopped trying to please everyone and instead sat down to think about what I desire? What if I had told my little sister how much I admire her and my brother how much I love him? One day, I made the perpetual decision that I wasn't going to spend my life wondering *what if*.

It was a Tuesday, much like any other. I was lying in my bed, listening to Taylor Swift sing her heart out about another love story gone wrong and diligently working on my Algebra II assignment. I looked up from my homework for a moment to pause my CD player- I can't concentrate on Cramer's Theory if I'm too busy rocking out to Taylor's catchy verses-and found myself staring straight into the mirror. At first glance, I looked pretty much the same as usual, but my eyes still lingered. I assessed my characteristic features: brown hair cascading in a mess of waves over my shoulder, side swept bangs covering my augmented forehead, blue eyes surrounded by MAC eyeshadow and softly curled eyelashes. However, the more I looked in the mirror, the clearer the image before me became. It was

like peeling back an onion, one layer at a time. My once bright eyes were now tired, the bags hidden behind porcelain foundation. My chubby, child-like cheeks, antecedently flushed with pink, were blanketed by shimmery blush.

The girl in front of me was serving a life sentence. She was hopelessly going through routine, daily motions: get up, go to school, do homework, eat, sleep, dream of nothing but white space. She was following The Plan, not her plan, but The Plan. The plan laid out by society for the normal people. School, college, job, marriage, kids, death. Nothing more, nothing less.

I realized that this was my entire life. I was seventeen years old and had left no room for surprises, love, utter despair, moments of bliss, silly mistakes, or tears of any kind in this conventional plan that I had so carelessly signed up for. At that moment, I knew that something had to change. The Plan needed to be remade. My way.

Pathetically enough, I didn't actually know how to make a list of what I wanted. I'd conformed so easily that I'd stopped dreaming big. I had stopped wishing for things at 11:11 and started wishing for A's on tests when a shooting star soared through the late night sky. After hours of contemplating an amalgam of personal ideas, I had an epiphany. The answer was right in front of me in my green spiral notebook. Writing. For as long as I can remember, I've been writing down everything. I've kept a journal from the time I was able to hold a pencil. Every tear, smile, and laugh was recorded in some ways in my writings. The best gift that anyone could give me was a new notebook and pencils. It only makes sense for someone like me to become a writer. What do writers do? They write books. Finally, I had the first real hope in years. From there, the ideas flowed out of me like steamy water from a shower head: unique colleges, a trip to Italy, writing a song, dance classes, a drastic hair cut, or even running a marathon, just to say I could do it.

I've finally found two definitions to life. Life can be a prison sentence covering the remaining portion of the offender's animate existence, or life can be the sum of experiences and actions that constitute a person's existence. There is no set list of experiences and actions to choose from. The possibilities are endless, even if you feel trapped by society's cold fate. I have a choice, and I choose not to serve a life sentence in this prison anymore.

Where I'm From

I am from another country,

from many differences and other habits.

I am from a big family,

from a narrow dining table and much to tell.

I am a little sister,

from a boy who looks like me, who is like me,

who sits next to me on the narrow table for dinner.

I am from nail polish and fashion magazines,

from bright colors and industry-chic,

from new hairstyles, gossip,

and every week another must-have.

I am a horse-friend,

from much work and much to see.

I'm from many adventures and getting up early,

from coffee with milk and shared hotel beds

after a tournament .

Despite all the stress,

I am from a wonderful place

with a wonderful family

and the best friends in this world.

I enjoy this life – every second, every day.

Poetry by Lina Hennig, Junior

Oil by Catrina Kroeger, Senior

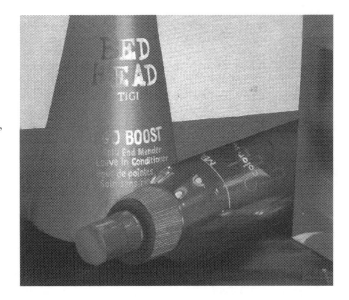

The Christmas Fire

Fiction by Rachel Kunnen, Sophomore
Watercolor by Jacob Kunnen, Senior

Lights flashing in every direction, people running at blinding speed. These were the things that greeted me on that cold and dismal Christmas morning.

It was four in the morning when I awoke to the sound of my pager going off and to the sound of Shelly, our dispatcher's voice, as she spouted off directions to the structure fire. Not bothering to change out of my pajamas I grabbed my coat and ran to my truck. Once inside I flipped my lights on, hoping to evade any people who were moronic enough to be out this early in the morning. I arrived on scene and watched as a beautiful three story house went up in a rage of fire. The windows had all been shattered due to the heat, and the ivory white paint had started to peel off, turning an unhealthy gray color as it did. Throwing on my gear, I ran to the engine and started pulling off hose lines, working as fast as I could without making a mistake. I could hear Henri telling me to start pumping water, and even though I didn't know where he was, I went back to the truck and started throwing valves. I watched as the lifeless hose sprang to life while Henri aimed it at the side of the house that was now completely engulfed in flames. Adrenaline was running through my veins, and I felt empowered, like I could do anything. But I knew my place. I knew that I couldn't do anything but man the trucks and hand out tools as needed. Still, I wished for my moment, my time to rise above what all the men thought of me simply because I'm

female. My time to rise up to the name my father set for me, As I looked up at the flames that continued to grow despite all our efforts, I saw him.

"Brian! Patrick! Michael! Someone!" I called out to the men, but no one paid me any attention. They were all lost in their tasks of fighting the fiery beast that was still growing. But I saw him. I saw the boy trapped in the house, the one that no one else thought to look for. I saw him. I look around frantically, trying desperately to find someone to help him, but no one was there. It was almost as if everyone else had disappeared, and as my vision focused in on him, I knew what I had to do. Running to the Heavy Rescue Truck, I grabbed an air tank and began to run towards the house. I slipped into it. No one noticed that I was gone; no one saw me go in.

Once inside the house all I could think about was the boy. *Find the boy. Where's the boy? Find the boy. Find the boy. Find the boy.* Above my head I heard a strangled cry of agony and fear. Running towards what remained of the staircase, I leapt with all my might, and I barely made it to the ledge of what was left of one of the upper steps. But I made it all the same. I had to use every ounce of my strength to pull myself up. Now on the second floor, I listened for a sound, any sound. Mentally I begged the boy

to make a noise, to say something, any sound. *Please make a sound! I need to hear you!* There it was, the faintest of pleas coming from the end of the hallway. I hurried down the hallway, treading as lightly as I could over the unstable floorboards.

Finally, I reached a door and grabbed the handle, preparing to pull the boy to safety. But wait; I knew that look to the fire. It was the calm before the storm. Back draft. Horrified at what might have been, I slowly backed away, knowing that there was nothing I could do. If I opened the door or broke through the wall, the sudden exposure of fresh oxygen would create an explosion of fire. The fire would come out of the opening, and trap us both in a flourish of flames. In the back of my head, I could still hear that nagging voice, the same one that coaxed me to find the boy, now wanting me to also help him. *Get the boy. Save the boy.*

Ignoring all my training, I threw open the door and burst through the flames. I landed on the floor, looking up to see him cuddled in a corner. He reminded me of a lost child in a supermarket. I made my way across the room as fast as I could. Once I made it to the boy, I threw myself over him to shield his body from the flames as they exploded into an insatiable inferno. When the explosion was over I took off my coat, wrapping him in it. Together we began what felt like a million mile journey to safety.

Once we were safely out of what I could only guess had once been his room, we huddled together and began to walk across the hallway. Seconds ago it was mostly intact, but the explosion left it damaged. It was showing signs of caving in now. Staying as close to the wall as we could, we made it down the hallway, only to be faced with the treacherous remains of the stairway. Glancing at the boy, I could see how blue his face was getting from trying to hold his breath. I slipped off my air tank, and put it on him, watching with relief as his face gradually gained its color under the soot that covered it. Making our way down the stairs seemed easy enough, until I heard the familiar moan of something giving way. We looked at each other as we fell. I reached for him and pulled him close, blocking his fall with my body. As we got up, the ceiling began to give way. We got up and sprinted to the door, making it outside the house and out of death's grasp once again. We collapsed as soon as we were out, and I thought that the danger was over.

Time seemed to stop. Everything slowed down, nearly to a complete standstill. Willing myself to keep going, I pulled him up with me as I stood and began to run. I don't know what made me continue, what pressed me on. I can only explain it as the voice of my father. It was as if I could hear him telling me to move, lifting me up

and pleading with me to move. The voice urged me to go anywhere, to move anywhere away from the house. The demon that was unleashed on the beautiful home had grown to its full strength. It now completely engulfed the home that everyone had envied, but it didn't stop there. The demon , greedier than ever, began to feed on the surrounding trees. I visually followed the path of the fire's arms as it reached for more, and I saw what it was grasping for. The gas tank.

Pulling the boy up again required all of my strength, but I pushed forward, screaming as I went. I told everyone to get as far away as possible. *Why aren't any of them moving? Why aren't they listening?* I continued to yell, silently willing all of my comrades to hear. After what seemed like centuries of yelling, someone finally looked at me. I pointed frantically at the gas tank, and watched as the realization hit the boy's face. He turned quickly, and started to yell to the others to run as the fire stretched to within inches of the gas tank. Still running, the boy and I made it to the

edge of his driveway when the explosion hit. It threw us forward, pitching us into the road. When I opened my eyes, all I could think about was the boy. *Where's the boy? Where's the boy? Where's the boy?* At last I spotted him. He was lying on a stretcher while paramedics scurried around him, caring for him. Laying my head down on the pavement once more, I let the exhaustion I had been fighting take over me as I fell into unconsciousness.

When I opened my eyes, I sat up in my hospital bed and tried to remember all that had happened on the night of the fire. All I could recall was seeing the boy going into the ambulance and knowing that he was going to be all right. When the nurse came for my routine checkup, I asked her to bring in the fire's official report, hoping it would bring back the memory of what had happened. As I read it, I found out that the boy's name was Jayden, and that he had been diagnosed with deafness three years earlier. If it hadn't been for his attempt at screaming for help, I would never have been able to find him. As for the other firefighters, no one was injured, and the surrounding houses had been saved. Setting the report on my bedside table, I closed my eyes and drifted off to sleep where I relived that cold and dismal Christmas morning in my dreams.

My Friend, *Frankie*

*Nonfiction by
Molly McGee,
Sophomore*

*Oil by Kimberly
Lord, Junior
Scholastic Art
Award Silver Key*

Growing up, I never had any friends. Maybe it was because I was shy. Maybe it was because I had to go to a special education school and ride what other people called the "retard bus" because I had epilepsy. Maybe it was the fact that people are just jerks. Whatever the case, I had a few school friends and a couple of after school people to hang out with. But no matter how hard I tried to like people, no one seemed to want to like me back. I would sit at the lunch table and wait, hopefully but in vain, for someone to sit with me. I was lonely and sad. I also got picked on a lot. I was called names, and in gym class, people would chase me around and throw dodgeballs at me and laugh. One hit me on the head so hard, it knocked my glasses off. That really hurt, and not just physically. In second grade when I cut my hair short, kids told me to stand in the boy's line. Another time someone threw silly putty in my hair, and Mrs. Bell had to cut a big chunk out of my hair that took a long time to grow back.

The only real friend I've had through the years can't even talk. But he listens. He has four legs, a long furry tail and his eyes are crystal blue. His name is Frankie, and he is a very special cat. We got Frankie when he was almost two years old, after someone dumped him off at our house. It was very special because he showed up about two weeks after we had to put our first cat, Ginger, to sleep because of cancer. When I first saw him sitting on our porch, he automatically started meowing and rubbing his body against our front door. I begged my dad to keep him, and at first he said "no," but after he stuck around for a couple of days he said "yes." We saw his big blue eyes and named him Frankie after Frank Sinatra. My dad didn't want to keep him inside because he sheds a lot, so he rests in our garage at night, and during the day he plays outside. It took him awhile to get use to us; he didn't like to be held or petted at first, but eventually he came to love us.

When he was younger, he would get into quite a bit of trouble. He got into a fight once with my neighbor's mean old cat, and he ended up rupturing a vein in his rump (it was hilarious when the vet had to shave his butt!), and he ruptured three veins in his ears, two in his left, one in his right. We were worried he would run away, so we got him a navy blue collar to make sure someone brought him back if he got lost. The next day he came back without it, and two weeks later our other neighbor found it stuck on a tree branch. Needless to say, Frankie hasn't worn a collar since then. I still keep it in a drawer in the garage.

In the spring he has loads of energy, and he'll scamper all around the yard like, well, a spring chicken. In the summer Frankie likes to chase me around when I try to pet him, but it's not too funny to me because his claws are sharp. In the fall he and I always take our annual picture of the two of us in a pile of leaves. I have all the pictures of the past years taped on my wall. In winter he loves to plow through the snow like a husky, and he is incredibly hard to find then because his fur is white. Through all the seasons, Frankie has been there for me when I needed a friend. He is the only person who really listens to me, and I can tell him all my secrets and never have to worry about him telling them to anyone else. He is my buddy, my best friend, my Frankie.

The Seasons of My Life

Poetry by Christina Newhart, Senior
Colored Pencil by Emily Thomas, Senior

I'm from applesauce and warm maple syrup
Sitting by the fire on a cold winter's night, listening to my grandpa talk
Watching the crops grow as I run through the fields
Drinking iced tea on the front porch watching a storm blow in
Walking down the street knowing everyone's name
Seeing the leaves change colors as I'm picking apples
Driving down an old country road with windows down blasting country music
Walking through the cold snow with my family to find that perfect Christmas tree
Playing fetch with my dog on a cool fall day
Catching fireflies on a warm spring night
Jumping into the lake with the sun beating down, listening to my cousins goof-around
Changing seasons
Winter, Summer, Spring, and Fall
Have filled my senses and my soul

Feeling Hope

Poetry by Ryan Ballinger, Junior

Photo by Emily Thomas, Senior

I am standing at the top of a magnificent
        waterfall,
Staring down it, hearing the water and feeling
        the breeze.
A great lake forms at the bottom and then a
        stream.
I follow the stream with my eyes and see it goes
        on forever.
I then look at the sky and gasp in sudden surprise;
The sunset is a beautiful and spontaneous sight.

I dive into the lake below the waterfall.
The water is warm and the wind is calm.
Lake serpents welcome me and show me their land,
Show me their kingdom, and their stream of gold.
I swim through the river with a warm, happy soul.

I stand at the top of the waterfall staring at the sky,
Taking in a deep breath and closing my eyes.
The wind blows my hair around and it is warm.
A tear rolls down my cheek and hits the stones.
I wish life was like a warm stream of hope.

Rain

Poetry by Chantell Cooper, Junior
Oil by Blake Harris, Senior

You hear the gentle pitter patter
As the rain lightly touches ground
You watch as the rain falls gently into the creek
A dozen rings dancing across the water
At the drops' disappearance
How can even one simple drop form such beauty
And yet be so small
The creek sounds so young
As it flows through the forest
This path it's chosen will never end
As its beauty blends with the tiny drops
The light filtering through the clouds
Through the canopy
Beautiful colors play on the water
The droplets of water joining in
It's as if they're playing a game
Laughing and enjoying each other's company
It happens so often
And yet so many do not see
How such beauty
Could exist and be so small and simple
The rain slowly stops
The ripples finishing the last steps
Of their natural eternal dance
The beauty leaves
But will soon come again

T O S S   A   P E N N Y

Nonfiction by Connor Berkebile, Senior
Photoshop Art by Emily Thomas, Senior

It begins at the wishing well. You throw a penny into the water at your hometown mall. The ripples whisper promises that your youthful innocence has no reason not to believe. You smile at the sight of the thousands of other wishes displayed in the depths of the artificial blue. The falsified color is just another lie you don't register. Your gaze passes over the sign denoting the charity to which the proceeds will be donated, but the look doesn't linger for long. Youth is impatient and loses interest easily. How captivating can a sign possibly be to a child?

Many years and life lessons later, you return to your hometown mall, and the well may be full of novel coins and contemporary wishes. Your gaze might chance over the sign once again. But experience has changed your perspective, and the look is now an enduring stare, a pondering inspection. You feel the weight of the change in your pocket and relieve it in the pool of hope, but your view remains on the sign. The scars from the brain tumor of your childhood tingle as you continue to stare at the name responsible for your persisting heartbeat. The ripples from the dropped change whisper a familiar promise, and you smile from the nostalgia. The tears running down your face into the falsely blue water seem an attempt to correct the lie. You have learned, through the course of your life, that not all wishes and dreams come true. However, peace fills your heart as you come to terms with that fact and realize not all wishes *have* to come true. Hoping doesn't save lives nearly as often as action. You frantically dash to your car, put the key in the ignition, and begin the short drive across your small town to the nearest bank. It ends at the wishing well.

Time Passages

Renga Poetry by Christina Newhart, Senior;
Cody Phillips, Junior; Emily Thomas, Senior;
Danielle Wroblewski, Senior; and Mariah Rippy, Junior

Sitting by the fire
listening to the grown ups
talk about the good old

times, and exchanging stories.
Being young and having fun,
our endeavors take us back

into the light again, remembering
my brother's hand and mine on a plastic flashlight.
Power outage, the storm takes

one light from us, but we make our own and find
our way along the darkened path,
looking for the place we need to be.

We never got lost when we were together.
Depending on one another
became a habit, and now we need to grow up.

NUCLEAR MELTDOWN

"In everyone's life, at some time, our inner fire goes out." - Albert Schweitzer

" I am ashes where once I was fire." - Lord George Gordon Byron

Futilely try to spark the dampened fires of loneliness, depression, and isolation...

Something Wrong

*Poetry Renga by Mariah Rippy, Junior;
Emily Kensinger, Senior; Emily Thomas, Senior;
and Kirsten Brown, Junior
Digital Art by Mariah Rippy, Junior*

Nobody knows why,
but the moon reflects my fire,
shining through trees,
alone and lingering.
They claim there's something
wrong with the way I

go about life.
Walking alone, standing alone
with no one to help me
but the spark inside,
the one that keeps me alive,
is lightened with

tears as they fall off my cheek.
I peer out behind bright eyes.
I am alone most days and
the one I call home
will never stargaze with

me in these fields.
So strange that one place
can hold so many memories.
The silence is heavy. Stars are
shining. And you are
nothing more than a memory.

Outside Looking In

Poetry Renga by Emily Kensinger, Senior;
Mariah Rippy, Junior; Kirsten Brown, Junior;
and Emily Thomas, Senior
Charcoal by Garrett Blad, Senior
Scholastic Art Award Gold Key

It's pitch black outside,
the night closing in on me.
Houses I pass are glowing with
loved ones inside and I stand on the outside

wondering if I'll ever be
a part of a family or ever just belong.
A bitter breeze soaks through
my clothing, clutching at

my thoughts and soul,
persuading me to walk away,
at least from this place.
The family notices

my presence briefly then turns back to dinner
as I cry and pull my threadbare
coat tighter, longing for the comfort
I have never known.

A Delicate Chain

Poetry by Ayla Felix, Senior
Charcoal by Ayla Felix, Senior

It's just a necklace with a broken chain.
Once upon a time it gleamed and glittered,
But its shine is now gone with age and dust.
She remembers wearing it,
Watching it catch the sun.
But she hasn't worn it for years,
Not since the delicate chain snapped.
Once upon a time it had been a gift
Wrapped in purple paper with a blue bow.
She remembers opening it,
Seeing the beauty for the first time.
His hands took it out and put it on her.
She remembers his fingers, so gentle,
Scrambling to close the tiny clasp.
He hasn't done that in years,
Not since he broke the delicate chain.
Once upon a time the beautiful trinket
Represented their love, their marriage.
She remembers wearing it with her white wedding gown
All those years ago.
But it hasn't meant anything for years,
Hasn't stood for a single thing
Since well before the delicate, golden chain broke.
And now it's just a necklace,
Gathering dust in a forgotten box.

I Will

Poetry by Ayla Felix, Senior
Photo by Kate Smith, Senior

Rain patters against the roof. It's loud.
"I'm leaving."
Thunder rumbles in the distance and the house quivers.
"I know."
A car goes by, lighting up the windows and the faces and the empty promises.
"Don't you care?"
The TV is on in the next room, but there's no one to watch it.
"Not anymore."
The windows leak a little.
"Why the hell not?"
Lightening flashes outside and it's one, two, thr——thunder roars.
"You've been gone for a long time."
Another car goes by, lighting up the room like the lightening, but in slow motion.
"Then you won't miss me."
The door shakes when it's slammed, and the little porcelain figures on the shelves threaten to fall.
"Oh, I will."

Night Dreams

Nonfiction by Sean Heckman-Davis, Senior
Photo by Karen Celmer, Senior

I don't have a car. This hasn't been much of a problem for me though, because my house is maybe two blocks from the high school. Needless to say, I walk home often. I don't particularly care for football games, but they are my favorite school event to walk home from. The reason for this is simple: I walk home from football games at night.

Night is my favorite time of day, despite how odd that sounds. I love listening to the sounds, or rather, the lack of sound that autumn nights provide. I walk on the sidewalk in front of the forest near the church across the street. As I move away from the game, everything calms down and shuts up, which to me, is the ultimate relief. The yells of success from scored touchdowns fade away and become the only source of sound in the entire night.

Unfortunately, I rarely remain the only one on my walks. Often, the sound is interrupted by cars and other vehicles. I've come to loath them immensely as time goes on. My beloved silence can be shattered in a second by a single vehicle driving past, with engine obnoxiously roaring in an effort to get wherever it thinks it needs to be. The worst ones play music. The "vroooom" I can tolerate in small amounts, but forcing me to listen to whatever stupid song they have blasting over their speakers is utterly despicable, in my mind. I realize that I am not the only person in the night, but why can't they?

To distance myself from those infernal contraptions, I often cut through the forest to get home. This is my favorite part of the walk. The trees muffle sounds even more, and everything that isn't seen in the day comes alive. I hear bats occasionally, and when it's early in the year and still warm, the sounds of crickets and cicadas provide background bliss. One night, a few years ago, I had the pleasure of walking through the forest with the fireflies. That was probably the closest thing I've ever had to a magical experience. The night was unusually warm on a Friday in mid-September, and fog was coming in. The sight of the fireflies, phosphorescent in the forest's night mist, was visually stunning. Each firefly was shining as brightly as it could in the effort to be noticed by the others, striving for personal contact. It was an experience I will not soon forget. I got home very late that night.

I don't have much hope that my forays into the nature of the night will continue at college. My planned choice of university is in the city, and I don't hold any doubts that the nightlife there will be at all similar to what I'm used to. "Cities never sleep" is sadly a cliché for a reason. I'll always remember the fun I had these past years, and when I come back on break, I plan to spend my time walking in the night.

⟦ Creative Sparks ⟧

Broken Puzzle

Poetry by Cody Phillips, Junior
Colored Pencil by Nick Havranek, Junior

I am from one puzzle broken into many pieces.
Like a frog jumping lily pad to lily pad,
I am from the darkness but I've made it to the light.
From being broke and starving to my belly always full,
I've morphed from the streets as my home
To always having somewhere to go.

I came from the shadows to a place of belonging,
From fighting these battles to signing the treaties.
The love that would hide has started to show,
No more picking sides when with juggalos.
I'm from being a stray with feelings tucked away.
I came from the mask that covers my face.

I came from the stars in the sky,
Different from humans, but I do not know why.
Elephants are in the room when I'm anywhere;
Where I'm from isn't earth for I don't fit in here.
The things that made me must not be physical

But things of magic for I am celestial.

Fiction by Jessica Verkler, Senior

CRUSHED BY BETRAYAL

Brrriiinng! The doorbell to my front door chimed. I raced towards the big, red rectangle, eager to see my old friend, London. She was home from college for Christmas break (just like I was), and we had agreed to hangout one day.

When I opened the door, London was standing there in a black wool coat. Her long, brown hair was flowing over her shoulders in waves. She smiled her perfect smile. I squealed, and we embraced in a giant hug. We had greeted each other like that for as long as I can remember.

I invited her in and took her coat. London kicked off her shoes and made a beeline for the kitchen. After hanging her coat in the closet, I followed. She was sitting at the island, eating one of my Christmas cookies. "You know I've tasted a lot of cookies in my 20 years, but yours are still the best," she smiled.

"Well, thank you. I've had a lot of practice. So tell me, is anything interesting going on in your life? How's college going for you?"

"It's fine. Nothing too exciting. I'm ready to be finished though."

We chatted for a few minutes about school, then I switched the topic. It was something I didn't like to ask about, but I had to know a few details.

"How are things between you and Jason?" I pried.

"Good. It's going well," London replied. "Have you seen the new <u>Alice in Wonderland</u> movie?"

Wow, she sure changed the subject fast, I thought. I didn't think it was that personal. I mean, can she blame me? She is dating my brother, after all. Occasionally, I want to know how things are going. It's easier to ask London than Jason.

London and Jason had started dating about two years ago. Jason was a senior in high school now, and London was a sophomore in college. We had all been surprised when they started dating, but they got along well, and it seemed like they were perfect for each other.

Suddenly, London's cell phone rang. She looked at it, and for a brief second I thought I saw a flash of fear go through her eyes. "Excuse me, I have to take this," she said stiffly. I watched her as she got up and stalked towards the living room.

After five minutes, she still wasn't back. I decided to get up and go pick out a movie for us to watch. I headed towards the living room, but then I stopped. London wasn't in the living room; she was in the laundry closet. I could hear talking. Odd, but I guess she just wanted privacy.

Soon London emerged, saw me standing there, and gave an embarrassed half-smile. I didn't ask any questions, except what movie she wanted to watch. We decided on The Hangover, because we wanted to laugh like crazy weasels. However five minutes into the movie, London's phone rang again. I paused the movie, she left to talk, and came back. I restarted the movie, but five minutes later, her phone rang again. She apologized, and I sat there waiting for her return. I wanted to ask who was calling. Something (I couldn't tell what) told me not to. The entire time London had been here, I'd noticed that she had been acting strange. She was jumpy, quiet, and seemed like she was trying to avoid something, although I had no idea what.

I turned to see London coming back into the room, and she looked frazzled. I could tell something wasn't right. "Is everything OK?" I asked.

She paused. "Yeah." Nothing else followed her one word answer.

"OK, well I was just wondering who was..." I didn't get to finish my sentence. For the fourth time in about twenty minutes, London's phone rang.

"I'll be back," she snapped. She stormed out of the room, and it almost seemed like she was mad at me. I felt like there was something London wasn't sharing with me. But what could it be? We always shared our problems with one another. We'd been best friends since elementary school; nothing was so bad that we couldn't confide in each other.

Before I could really think about it, I got up from the couch and tiptoed to the door leading out to the hallway. I saw London go around the corner and head up the stairs. She didn't go all the way up though. I heard her stop near the top; I guess she thought I was listening in. Then she started talking.

"WHY do you keep calling?"

"Look, if I couldn't give you an answer five minutes ago, what makes you think I can give you one now?"

"Chazz, I'm hanging out with his sister. This is a horrible time."

OK, who is she talking to? And why are they mentioning my brother and I?

"Yes, it feels awkward."

"What?"

I saw her expression warp. She looked like a concerned animal.

"How do you expect me to choose? This is a really difficult decision. We've been dating for two years."

Wait...what? What is she talking about?

"Chazz, I know what I told you, but I just can't find the right time to do it. I still care about him.

"I have enjoyed our time together, but it feels...wrong. Hanging out with you won't feel right until I iron out this problem."

Problem... is she talking about Jason?

"Soon. I'm home for Christmas. I will talk to him when I see him."

Oh crap.

"Of course he's going to be upset! We've been dating almost two years. But being away from him...It's not the kind of relationship I want."

No, London. This isn't like you.

She paused, a slight smile playing at her mouth, then she said, "You're the kind of guy I've always wanted."

The final nail in the coffin. I slowly dragged myself back to the living room, unable to believe my ears. It felt like *I* was getting dumped. I could see the pain in Jason's eyes already. It didn't seem real. London...she had always preached about loyalty in relationships. Well I guess there's a hypocrite in all of us. How long had she been seeing "Chazz" behind my brother's back? How much time did they spend together? More importantly, what did they do when they were together? I sat down, trying to decide what to do. Should I confront her? Or just let it go? I told London when they started dating that if she ever broke up with him, I wouldn't hold it against her. But this was different. I didn't know how close she and this guy already were, but either way, it sounded like they had a thing going on between them. And she was still dating my brother. I couldn't believe her.

The door opened. London walked in and sat on the couch, acting like nothing had happened. "Are we going to watch the movie?" she inquired.

It didn't matter what I said . After tonight, our friendship would never be the same. "Oh, we will," I sighed, "but first, let's talk about this problem that needs to be ironed out."

Spilt-Spaghetti Life

Poetry by Autumn Ladyga, Senior
Charcoal by Nick Havranek, Junior

Your smile so flipped,
Like maybe your life slipped
From under your flamingo legs,
While your weeping willow heart begs,
For a chance to recover
Instead of suffer.
Your rainbow life took a turn for the worst,
And now your diamond mind thinks that you're cursed.
You now begin to change into a denim person
You used to be so unique, but now you only worsen
Cleaning up your spilt-spaghetti life seems impossible,
But I will always be here because I feel responsible.

You Disappeared Again

Poetry by Danielle Wroblewski, Senior

You disappeared again.
Where did you go?
I'm sitting in this empty room
Writing you a letter you'll never read.

I wonder what
You are thinking?
Are you thinking about how
You left me with little but misunderstanding?

I'm curious, what
Are you doing, darling?
Are you realizing that you made
The wrong choice, listened to the wrong words?

Tell me, why did you
Let this happen to us?
Did I not love you enough,
Not care for you as deeply as necessary?

I need to know, what
Did I do so wrong as to make you leave?
Was being myself not good enough,
Was there another who holds your heart?

Where did you go?
You disappeared,
Again.

Bando Blues

Poetry by Emily Thomas, Senior
Scratchboard by Emily Thomas, Senior
Scholastic Art Award Gold Key

I woke up this morning
before the sun was out
I woke up this morning
gotta play my sax loud
Contesting next week, and the brass line still sucks
If we don't march well, we'll be shoot outta luck

I've got the bando blues
I'm sick of four in the morning
I've got the bando blues
Soaked to the bone, the rain is pouring
Box drill, slides and stop signs
I think I'm going outta my mind
I've got the bando blues

Sectionals before practice
Verbal abuse 'till then
Sectionals before practice
Crap! Next week is Penn
I wanna go to state,
but I feel like I'm too late
I've got the bando blues

I've got the bando blues
I'm sick of four in the morning
I've got the bando blues
Soaked to the bone, the rain is pouring
Box drill, slides and stop signs
I think I'm going outta my mind
I've got the bando blues

"Eights and Eights!" he calls
and then the seniors start to yell
"Eights and Eights!" he calls
I think I'd rather be in hell
If marching band doesn't kill me soon
then I don't know what else will do
I've got the bando blues

I've got the bando blues
I'm sick of four in the morning
I've got the bando blues
Soaked to the bone, the rain is pouring
Box drill, slides and stop signs
I think I'm going outta my mind
I've got the bando blues

A Cry For The Children

Poetry by Amy VanderVelden, Senior
Pencil by Seth Barkman, Senior

Once upon a time you played
You laughed
In your eyes everyone was equal
Why are you here
Little children
You never asked for this
What could you have possibly done
Why were you ripped out of the arms
Of your loving parents
What did you do
Did you see your parents
Thrown into the fire
Are you now
All alone
No one to tell you
It will be all right
No longer able to hold you through
The cold nights
Did you wish your future goodbye
You will never know it
But you used to have one
Do you stare at the entry arches
Through which you will join
Family as mingled smoke
Are you afraid
Or do you not yet understand
When it is all over
Will the world finally see
How the cry of the children
Will finally be set free

Incomprehension

Poetry by Chantell Cooper, Junior
Charcoal by Dillynn Schleg, Sophomore

From a stormy day
To a dreary night
Clouds roll in as others drift out
A night of dreams
And a day of fear
Hear the thunder crack
As the clouds roll over one another
Receive a glimpse of a face in the moon
Only visible for a second
Disappearing beyond understanding
Incomprehensible whispers
Enticing and alluring those further
Those no one will ever see again
Clearing a conscience once forgotten
A world unknown to all
A world without understanding
A world without knowledge
Forget now all that has been taught
Words whispered never again
Answers sought and never granted
Forget now all once known
Never again return
This night forever more
Done now
Whispers fading
Trapped forever
A world with only one name
A place never dreamed of
In rejection since the dawn of time
Hell

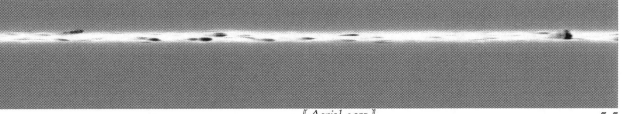

I
RUN

Fiction by Megan Beery, Senior
Oil by Ayla Felix, Senior
Scholastic Art Award Silver Key

JEALOUS. I can see my sister

flitting and fluttering around her kitchen, her happy singing filling the house. We're full blooded sisters, but we're as different as two blue eyed blondes can be. She has sun kissed golden hair that's usually spun up into a messy bun. She wears no jewelry, apart from her wedding band on casual days, and even during formal events, she wears few extra adornments. I watched as her gray eyes filled with a nurturing affection whenever she looked at Noel, her three-year-old daughter.

Dinner was well underway, but it's hard to prepare a meal while helping a toddler eat. I'm completely useless when it comes to cooking, but as far as helping Noel eat, I felt confident in my capabilities. Olivia's soft, loving eyes left Noel's for a moment as the oven timer beeped for her attention. She left Noel sitting at the small island while she tended to the food that needed to be removed from the oven. Moving deeper into the comfortable kitchen centered around the island, I slid onto the tall stool next to Noel's. When I nestled in close to the child for a hug, I caught her scent. I noticed how much it was like Olivia's scent. My little sister had always had what I described as the "baby scent" Not the smell of old

ON THE
WIND

formula and dirty diapers, like a day care center, but more like the scent of a newborn's scalp. To me it smelled innocent and kind, just like my unassuming little sister. Noel's wasn't exactly the same; her's had an earthy, growing tone to it, but it was innocent like Olivia's. Noel struggled against me, looking up at me with her mother's eyes. Unlike her mother's eyes, though, Noel's bore a mistrustful glint to them while they were focused on me. She looked at me like she could see the gypsy inside of me, barely contained and fighting to get out once again. Pulling away from her, I sat up and looked over her neon green plate. She had a matching sippy-cup with various farm animals cartooned over it. She'd barely picked at her chicken nuggets, and her green beans had gone completely untouched.

"Why don't you try your veggies, Noel?" I asked her, trying to make my voice as soothing as possible.

"They're ukey," she complained, tossing her golden blonde hair back in a way that reminded me very much of Olivia.

"Not with the ," I lowered my voice and shielded my lips from Olivia by cupping a hand over my lips, making it a game for Noel, "secret ingredient."

Noel looked at me doubtfully, yet intrigued all the same. I rose and went to Olivia's stainless steel side-by-side refrigerator. It looked like an out of place rhinoceros in her otherwise quaint, country styled kitchen. Opening it, I rooted around until I found what I was searching for. Removing a mostly empty bottle of Parmesan cheese, I closed the refrigerator door and returned to my niece. Hiding the cool container behind me with one hand, I slid back onto the stool next to Noel's. She studied me. My stormy, dark blue eyes and thick eyeliner must have seemed very strange

to her, being that both of her parents had temperate blue grey eyes. She chewed on a chicken nugget, more effectively drooling on it than actually consuming it, as her eyes continued to roam over my face. Olivia cast an amused look our way, relieved from the responsibility of Noel for a moment. I don't like children as a rule, but Noel was fun to be with most of the time.

"Close your eyes," I instructed covering her eyes with my left hand, just in case she decided to peek. "The secret ingredient is top secret, so I can't let anyone else know what it is," I explained, doubting if she'd understand.

I popped open the sprinkle side of the lid and scattered powdery clumps of white cheese over her green beans. When I was finished, I uncovered her eyes to find that she hadn't closed them at all. Rebellious little imp. Leaning down, I set the container on the cornflower blue and white linoleum floor. When I righted myself once more, Noel was looking at her newly seasoned vegetables curiously. Taking her plastic fork, I slipped the chunky tines into one of the beans and lifted it to her lips. A few bits of cheese fell off the bean and into Noel's lap as I verbally coaxed her

to open her mouth. She looked around for her mother, desperation evident in her eyes. Olivia kept her back towards Noel, aware of the situation but preoccupied with the meal that she was preparing. I heard her slip a cookie sheet into the oven as I tried to entice Noel to open her mouth. Olivia set the timer on the oven and glanced over her shoulder at her stubborn daughter.

"Noel, just one bite. We try everything once, remember?" Olivia's gentle voice did more than all my cajoling had accomplished.

Noel opened her mouth slightly, barely wide enough for me to slip the green bean in and get the fork back out. She refused to look at me as she chewed slowly, trying to be defiant in her compliance. When at last she finished the single green bean, she reached forward with one pudgy little hand to grasp another one. I arched my brow at Olivia, who simply laughed quietly to herself.

"Are they still 'ukey'?" I asked Noel.

"Ukey!" she proclaimed, eating the entire portion, one Parmesan covered green bean at a time.

I heard the front door open as Olivia's husband and Fyre came into the house. They'd gone to the store

for a few items that Olivia needed for dessert, but I honestly don't know why she trusted Delvin to do her grocery shopping. I've spent the last two years reconciling with my family and trying to get my life straightened out. During that time I've gotten to know my sister's family very well, and in all that I've learned, the fact that Delvin is incredibly culinarily impaired stands out above all else. I've been spoiled by Fyrefly, in that he loves to cook and experiment with new tastes. I'm certain, that without Fyre, Delvin would have completely muddled the list that Olivia gave him. Fyre called out my name and a brief greeting as he entered the kitchen. He set the brown paper shopping bags on the white, marbled countertop next to Olivia. Delvin followed Fyre in, silently brushing a kiss over Olivia's cheek as he began to unpack the bags that Fyre had set down. Delvin busied himself with stocking the cornflower blue cupboards in his almost constant silence. I had always wondered what kind of man could handle my sister's constant sporadic, jubilant energy. Delvin, in all his quiet masculinity, provided her perfect opposite and her perfect match.

"The lasagna is done, and there's only a few minutes left on the garlic bread," Olivia said as she began to remove a large, glass mixing bowl from a corner cabinet. "Do you mind setting the table?"

She looked directly at me, giving the impression that it was more of an instruction than a request. Nodding, I removed four white porcelain plates from the cabinet over the sink while Fyre collected the silverware that we would need from a drawer. Leaving the kitchen, I entered the dining room. It featured a blond wood table and large windows, giving a very open air feeling to the room. It was almost as if it was meant to be a three season sunroom, rather than an actual part of the house. The room was painted a very mellow pastel orange, and the color gave the room a warm, comfortable tone. After setting the plates down, I returned to the kitchen through an open archway that connected the two rooms. Delvin was cleaning Noel up, as it would be time for her to go to bed soon. I also noticed that someone had put away the container of cheese that I'd left on the floor. Maneuvering around Olivia, I found the cabinet where drinking glasses were kept, and I took four out. After adding them to the table, I did my best to stay out of Olivia's way. She was quickly creating what I guessed to be a French silk pie. Fyre and I left the kitchen, going out the screen door onto the screened in back porch. Looking over the set of white wicker furniture that adorned the porch, I chose a love seat covered in floral print pads. Settling comfortably into the love seat's contours, I looked at the other pieces in the wicker set. There were a couple of matching chairs and a table that helped to complement the charming area. Fyre eased down next to me, leaning back against the woven wood. He closed his eyes and breathed quietly, perfect exactly as he was. I watched as golden and red leaves were caught by the breeze, leaping and dancing over the lawn until they were trapped by the chain link fence. Little bits of leaf flew like nature's confetti through the air. They were light enough to ride the wind up to the neighbors' roofs, where they dusted the dark shingles with vibrant colors.

Suddenly, I was back on campus, leaves blowing through the air. They were everywhere. The scent of fall played among my friends and I, toying with strands of our brightly colored hair as it ran with the wind. We'd just left our dorms after supplementing our senses; the urge to be outside had been too great to overcome. We were laughing and falling over each other, more for the sensation that physical contact brought than the actual inability to walk correctly. I saw black; we were all dressed in black, dripping bright greens, vibrant purples, cool blues and deep, entrancing reds. Safety pins riddled our clothes and skin, piercing jackets, bags and ears. One girl even had a pin through her lower lip, and I thought she was insane. At the same time I envied her for the reckless abandon that it had taken to do that.

We found our way to a fountain, tall and made of smoothed concrete blocks. We were entranced by the water, its texture and all the colors in the mist given off by the toppling water. A couple of the guys began to roughhouse, shoving and bumping into one another. I laughed along with the others; it was such beautiful, innocent play. We were all beautiful in that moment. Our dog tags, gauges and spiked accessories shone in the dusk evening light, giving off the most alluring reflections of the shifting figures. Playing around the fountain. The kind of reflections that you don't want to look away from because they're better than what they're reflecting. I heard a splash as one of the guys fell into the fountain. Turning to look at him, I saw the water washing over him as he lay on his back beneath the surface. He ran his hands through the water, and I could see his enjoyment in the way he opened his eyes to watch the water move over his hands. My cell phone rang, and when I answered it, Fyre's voice came through the small speakers. He asked me to come to his dorm because he wanted to go out to dinner that night. Without a word to my fixated friends,

I left them to go to Fyrefly. As I walked away, I heard splashing from the fountain. The boy's voice was distraught, garbled with water. It sounded as if he was trying to get out of the fountain. As I walked away, a sense of dread came over me. I didn't look back at my friends, though. I began to run. Using the wind as a force to aid my speed I ran on it, lighter than the leaves that it carried.

Gasping, I blinked several times before my sister's porch became clear once more. Looking around, I saw that Fyre was still relaxing against the couch with me, his hands clasped behind his head for support. Leaning forward, I let my head fall into my open palms. Massaging my temples, I began to calm down. I could feel my heart rate begin to slow as I assured myself that no one knew. Not a living soul knew that I'd been there that evening. Fighting back the fear from my flashback, I tried to convince myself that I was safe now. Nobody knew. Tragically, the boy who'd fallen into the fountain died that night. He drowned, either by his own fixation with the water or by the hands of the other guys. In court they had testified innocent, insisting that that they'd done nothing to keep him underwater. I thought that I knew otherwise, but how could I be certain? I couldn't testify against them, even if I'd been sure that they had killed him. After all, according to the record I wasn't even at the scene. Fyre was my alibi; he said that I'd been with him at the time of the death, and with footage of me going into his dorm, who was to say otherwise? We'd stayed on campus that night, rather than going out as Fyre had wanted to. I was so high that I'd have made a scene if we'd gone anywhere. My friends were all charged with varying degrees of blame for the boy's death. At least two of the guys are in jail for life, and a couple more were charged with a few years for possession of illegal substances. All of them went to rehab, and I suppose they're doing fine now. To be honest, we lost contact after that. I haven't seen any of them since we were all in that courtroom together. After that I began to lose myself to any drug I could find, rather than simply Ecstasy, as I'd done before. Before, it'd been more of a social thing, just to relax and have fun. Those days, I was lucky to go

Photo by Kim Lord, Junior

two days without using. I eventually dropped out of school, and got a part time job as a third shift cashier at the local grocery store. My parents threw me out when I quit school, so I moved in with Fyre. He was more sympathetic towards my condition, blaming it on grief over my friends. I let him believe it was grief, rather than guilt, that aided in my downfall. To this day he doesn't know that I was there, that I watched the boy drown as I stood next to all my friends.

"Dinner!" I heard Olivia call from inside the kitchen.

I sat up and looked out over the backyard once again. I watched as

a few scarlet leaves rode the wind across the lawn before I felt Fyre stir next to me. Turning my attention to him, I looked into his warm, caramel eyes. He stood and offered me his hand. Taking it, I let him help me up, and we went to have dinner with Olivia and Delvin.

"When are you going to call your parents?" Fyre asked me as he unlocked the front door to our condo.

"Not yet. When I'm sure, I suppose," I replied, brushing past him as he held the door open for me.

"Sure of what, love? You've been clean for almost a year and a half now. Don't you think they're concerned about you? Don't you want to know how they're doing?" He followed me in, pulling the door closed behind himself.

"I want to be completely certain that I'm not an addict anymore, that I've got this kicked. Besides, Olivia tells me what they're up to every time we get together." Removing my calf length jacket, I tossed it onto the couch and made my way to the stairs on the other side of the living room.

"It's been a year, five months and eighteen days since you took a hit. Isn't that enough time to be officially drug free?" He followed me up the stairs and into the full bathroom across from our bedroom.

I didn't answer him, silently fuming. I found the bottle of makeup remover and poured some onto a tissue. Dabbing my eye shadow away, I seethed at Fyrefly as he leaned against the open door frame. Who was he to tell me that I was over my problem? I was still fighting demons that he was completely unaware of. I watched him as he removed his cell phone from its holster at his hip. I watched as he dialed on its touch screen surface and held the phone to his ear. After a couple of seconds, his face lit up in a devilish grin.

"Hey, dad. How are you doing?" he asked of the phone, listening as his father responded. "We're fine. We just got back from having dinner with her sister. Do you have any lunch plans this week?" I watched as he stared directly at me, making his point clear. "Tuesday is great. I'll see you around noon, then? Take care, dad."

"I get it, Fyre; you've got a great relationship with your parents. Well, I don't, okay?" I all but screamed at him, fighting my tears back, "My parents threw me out when I needed their support most. My family is just not like yours."

"That's all I'm asking for. No heart to heart confessional or even a deep conversation at all. Just a, 'Hi, how are you doing? By the way, I've been living forty five minutes away from you for the past four years, during which time you were wondering where I'd run off to.' Just make a connection with them, love."

Wiping my eyeliner away next, I hid my tears by dabbing them up as I removed my makeup. I glared at him in the mirror as he met my gaze with unwavering golden brown eyes. I admired his black hair; it was straight, waving into gentle ringlets at the tips. I loved his thick black hair, especially since it contrasted with my wavy, silver blonde hair so well. Dropping the used tissue into a waste basket beside the vanity, I reached for another one and moistened it with the makeup remover. Using long, gradual arcs, I removed my foundation, leaving my skin bare. Tossing the second tissue into the waste basket as well, I opened a drawer and put the makeup remover into it before pushing it closed with more force than was absolutely necessary. I felt Fyre's skin as he wrapped his arms around me, burrowing his face in the tender down at the nape of my neck.

"What's wrong, love? What aren't you telling me?" he whispered softly, his full lips caressing my skin.

"I had another one today," I murmured quietly, ashamed.

"At Olivia's house?"

"Yes," I answered, melting into his embrace.

"While Delvin and I were at the store?" His voice was concerned. What would Olivia have thought if I'd had a flashback while helping her with Noel?

"No, while we were on the porch," I told him.

He stepped back from me and leaned down to scoop me into his arms. Cradling me, he carried me across the hall and into our bedroom. Depositing me on our bed, he sat next to me.

"I'm sorry, love. I know how much those upset you, but there's really nothing you can do to prevent them. They're from your past, and they're a part of who you were, not who you are." He wrapped an arm around me as I cuddled against his side. "What do you think induced it?"

"The leaves. I saw the way the wind blew them along, and it reminded me of when I would run on it," I explained.

Markers by Ashley Navilliat, Senior

"You run with the wind, but you can't run on it, just the same as walking through walls. You run into them, love," he patiently reminded me.

"It doesn't feel that way, and honestly, the experience was always worth the bruises I got. I know I can't walk through walls, but believing that I can is more enjoyable than knowing the truth," I told him.

"If it makes you happy, I don't care what you believe." He sounded like he was tired of the subject as he shifted into a more upright position.

"How did you break away so easily?" I asked him. "You enjoyed the highs as much as I did."

"You're right. I did enjoy them, but they were holding me back. My erratic behavior was keeping me from promotions at work and stealing my quality time with you. So I quit cold turkey. It wasn't easy." He stood up, looked at me affectionately and brushed my side bangs back from my face. "But every time I look at you I know that it was worth it."

Leaning down, he pressed his lips against my forehead. Brushing his cheek against mine, he wrapped me in a warm embrace. When he stood once more, he turned and walked into the bathroom, closing the door behind him. I heard him turn on the water, waiting for it to heat up so he could shower. His words of encouragement meant a lot to me. Really, they did. It didn't change the fact that I wanted to run on the wind, though. Getting off my bed, I opened the drawer on my bedside table. Removing a syringe, I set it on the tabletop as I searched for the little glass bottle of liquid that I'd left there. It was missing. Not to be deterred, I went to my closet, where I'd hidden some in one of my old purses. Opening the closet door, I stood on the tips of my toes to reach the top shelf where all of my old purses were kept. Pulling down a leather one, I cast it aside. It wasn't the one I was looking for at the moment. The next one was black and white stripped, and I knew that I'd found what I was looking for. Reaching inside the main pocket, I found a small side zipper pocket and unzipped it, feeling for the small glass bottle that I'd left there, only to find that it was empty as well. Throwing both purses back into the closet, I closed it and continued my search. Fyre had known about my first hiding spot, and he second one wasn't hard to guess. Leaving my room, I went downstairs and found my way through the dark hallway into my studio. Flicking on the light switch, I went to a table where I kept all my supplies. A basket contained all my small bottles of paints, oils and, with any luck, a bottle of my precious liquid. Rummaging around in the basket, I was shocked to find that the bottle I'd hidden in it was missing as well.

"Thief," I hissed under my breath, my anger with Fyre renewed.

Pulling my blue cell phone out of my right front pocket, I looked through my contacts for my old dealer's number. I hadn't called him in some time, and I didn't even know if he was still in the business, but it was worth a shot. His name wasn't there, as in, erased from my phone's memory. Cursing softly under my breath, I looked for someone else. I didn't buy from her as often as I had from my dealer, but she'd saved me before when I had been in a pinch. Predictably, her number was gone, too. Replacing my phone in the pocket of my stonewashed jeans, I left my studio, turning off the lights as I walked out. Entering the living room, I picked up my long black jacket from where it lay on the couch. Slipping it on, I opened the front door and crept out, closing it silently behind me. I didn't know where I was going, I just went. Starting at a conservative jog, I made my way along rows of condos similar to the one that I shared with Fyre. Soon I was out of the development and on a street leading out of the city and into the suburbs. I could feel the wind at my back as it carelessly tousled my hair and whipped at the edges of my jacket. The blacktop felt good under my feet as I pounded against it consistently. I remember the way that running had been like a drug to me in high school and even through college. I began to wonder why I'd ever left this sport, this therapy. I lost myself in the steadiness of my own breathing. I inhaled, staggered my exhale, waited a moment, inhaled, staggered my exhale, and repeated. Picking up my speed, I ran with the wind along the quiet, curvy road. I wasn't certain exactly what direction I was headed. The speed felt good, and with the breeze at my back, I lost the sensation of my feet against the pavement. I couldn't feel the air going into and out of my lungs. I glided over the ground

like a thick fog rolling in for the night. I felt like I was running on the wind again. This is what I'd been craving: the feeling of utter weightlessness, the loss of all my inhibitions and concerns. I felt as if nothing else mattered now. There was only the wind and I, only the way I rode a breeze over the road. I ran on the wind until I gasped for air, needing more than my body could give me. I slowed to a jog again to catch my breath. I knew then that I didn't need the drugs to feel high. I knew that this was the only high that I'd ever need. By now my anger had dissipated, so I turned back toward home and rode the wind the whole way.

"Where did you go?" Fyre asked as I lay down next to him.

"I went for a run," I whispered back, kicking off my tennis shoes and pushing them off the side of the bed.

"Did you run on the wind?" he asked, his deep voice muddled by the effects of sleep.

"Yes," I answered softly, nestling against his back, inhaling his warm scent. I knew that come what may, this was all I'd ever truly need.

Staying off the drugs isn't easy. It's the hardest thing I've ever done, to be honest with you. Every time I feel like I can't handle it and that I need a fix right away, I go for a run. It helps me feel free, and it takes all the stress off my mind. When I look at my sister's family and the life that she has, I know that she's got it good. Because of her, I know that someday I want to marry Fyrefly and have a child of my own. I want to be able to nurture it and help it grow. As long as I stay clean, my future dreams and ambitions are within reach. I have no reason to be ashamed of my past. Even though Olivia's life might be more conventional there's nothing of hers for which I am jealous.

Old Heart, New Day

Poetry by Connor Berkebile, Senior
Photo by Kate Smith, Senior

I stare off with an old heart
at an amorphous horizon.
The morning sun glimmering
just above the conjunction
of the heavens and the earth
seems to be my guide.
I long for an escape,
a taste of adventure,
and a fresh beginning
in a place where nobody
knows my name or sees
the force behind every smile.
The royal ground I stand upon
sings of the memories
and experiences of
the girl I once was.
The suitcase next to me is empty,
for I am leaving myself behind.
My feet are like the wings
of a hummingbird
restless in anticipation
of the long journey ahead.
I take a certain step towards uncertainty
but indecisiveness takes over,
and I hesitate before
embarking upon another.
I look back at my shadow
stretched across the dew-covered
grass of the morning.
In the midst of the gloom
of my former life
stands a pair of feet,
but I refuse to raise my view.
I turn on the spot, and
leaving my shadow and its components behind,
sprint off towards the rising sun
and the unknowns the new day will bring.

Brushes on Canvas

Poetry by Kirsten Brown, Junior
Pencil by Hannah Bottorff, Sophomore

Cheap green shades
Scraped up walls
Feeble sun
Still he calls

Brushes on canvas
Colors on air
Curve of her body
Flow of her hair

Deeper than silence
Feelings he fought
Louder than screaming
A moment is caught

A gift sent from heaven
He still feels like hell
His beautiful dream
Elle est tres belle

The world of the artist
Is dismal at best
Fleetingly filled with beauty
Life's greatest jest

A Closed Shell

Poetry by Jessica Verkler, Senior
Charcoal by Kaylee Bruggeman, Sophomore

I get in my car,
the engine roars at me.
I punch the radio and a song about hope and better days comes on.
Not what I want to hear.
———BZIIIPPPP! ———
The radio is turned off.
A passenger pigeon, I follow the familiar route
to family, to home and get out.

Like a scared octopus, the sky has released its inky blackness of night.
The cool breeze licks
my face
and turns my tears
to miniscule glaciers.
I search the sky for some remote answer
but get nothing from it.
Even the twinkling stars laugh at me.

Like a tidal wave crashing onto Waikiki,
I throw myself atop my comforter.
The name fits it well.
And like a hermit crab,
I burrow under the covers and
hide from the world.
But my feelings of inadequacy
creep in and find me.
They never let me rest.

Never the best;
always a step behind.
I want something that defines me
and makes me something special.
I'm still waiting to break out of my oyster.
What I do, what I accomplish
is topped by someone so much better than I.
I want to stand apart.

As my face rests on a soothing pillow,
I try to comprehend who I am
and wander through a forest of unease.
I will always be in the Shadow of All,

Just Once

Poetry by Alexandria Drzewiecki, Junior
Charcoal by Hannah Bottorff, Sophomore
Scholastic Art Award Honorable Mention

Just once I'd like to be true to myself

Just once I'd like to not feel alone

Just once I'd like to not be ashamed of who I am

Just once I'd like to feel like I can trust again

Just once I'd like to feel safe

Just once I'd like the pain to subside

Just once I'd like to not be just another voice in the crowd

Just once I'd like my song to be heard

Just once I'd like someone to grab my hand when I'm reaching for help

Just once I'd like my wish to come true

Just once I'd like to be the protected and not the protector

Just once I'd like to shine in your eyes

Just once I'd like to open my locket and have my eyes stay dry

Just once I'd like to hear the words "I love you"

Pride

Poetry by Chloe Jacobson, Senior
Watercolor by Ariel Rensberger, Senior

They stare at me
hoping to see right through,
as if I am not there,
but I shall hold my own.
On this bus I shall stand
and hold my head up high,
with pride for my race
and disdain for the society
where I am not welcome,
yet I am still here.
My ancestors worked for their freedom
giving me my right
to assert that self-same privilege.
But as I fix my eyes out the window,
I notice a sea of white,
white cars, white sidewalks,
white ads, white people,
yet we are the ones that have history here, too.
My blood is planted in this ground;
my knees have worked it
since I was a child. Blame us for
your prosperity and good fortune,
and then tell us that in your country
we are not born equal.
How can you tell us that our children
are not fit to touch your skin,
that what is ours and what we have are
good enough to suffer and bleed for this country
but not good enough
to lay equal claim to what we are dying to receive:
the right to live equally,
the freedom to walk down the streets and
not be forced back into proverbial slavery.
This is our time!
My children will one day sit with your children
in peace and harmony,
all equally free.

Faith Enough for Me

Nonfiction by Kelsey Mitschelen, Senior
Pencil by Kirsten Brown, Junior

"Kelsey time to get up for church," my dad whispered into my room one Sunday morning. After he left, I jumped up and quickly got dressed in my finest clothes. I ran downstairs, ate a quick breakfast, grabbed my bible, and galloped out the door. We drove to church and picked a seat in the center of the pew.

The song leader began with out opening hymnal, "I Will Praise Him Hallelujah." I sang along feeling close to the Lord. That was the first time I ever heard that song. I was about ten years old, and I was in church. After the song ended, we all sat down and the preacher came on stage and told us to open our bibles. We spent an hour praising God and listening to his message.

"Kelsey, get out of bed right now or I'm going to drag you out of bed!" my dad yells into my room. I pretend to get up, but as soon as I hear the stairs creak under his feet, I crawl deeper under the covers. Like Alice in Wonderland, I fall deep into the rabbit hole. Ten minutes later my dad comes storming into my room with a cup of ice water, threatening to pour it on me. I reluctantly scramble out of bed. My dad leaves, and I get dressed in my favorite skinny jeans and a t-shirt with the name of my favorite band on it. With slumped shoulders, I walk downstairs, right past my dusty bible, and I am forced out the door to go to church.

We take our usual seat in the center of the pew.

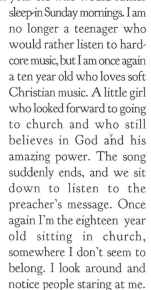

Praise Him Hallelujah." I refuse to sing along. It's been eight years since I last heard that song, and the familiar words float through my head. And then it all comes back. I am no longer an eighteen year old who would rather sleep in Sunday mornings. I am no longer a teenager who would rather listen to hardcore music, but I am once again a ten year old who loves soft Christian music. A little girl who looked forward to going to church and who still believes in God and his amazing power. The song suddenly ends, and we sit down to listen to the preacher's message. Once again I'm the eighteen year old sitting in church, somewhere I don't seem to belong. I look around and notice people staring at me. Most of them are women in long skirts shaking their heads disapprovingly at my choice in clothes. My eyes drop , but I can still feel their eyes on me like lasers shooting into me, cutting me in half. It's strange how much I have changed since I was ten. Not just my looks but my spirituality, too. I know its not how my parents wanted me to be, but this is who I am. I may not be a preacher when I'm older, but at

The Mental Image of You

Poetry by Janay Crane, Sophomore
Charcoal by Seth Baker, Senior

I haven't slept since we last spoke,
or maybe I'm in a dream and haven't awoke.
I'm not sure who I am or how I feel
or what part of you is pretend and what is real.
Could my mind paint pictures as vivid as these;
if you understand, could you tell me, please?
Because I could have sworn that I saw love in your eyes
like stars that shine in the late night skies.
I only hope they shine for me.

But am I even worthy of the smallest admiration?
To ruin your innocence would be an abomination.
You're a lamp of hope in a raging sea,
or are you but a mirage out to mock me?
So don't you dare watch me as I walk away,
and don't you dare miss me since I can't stay,
but even if you do, hold that secret dear,
because I'm trying to save you from one more tear.
If I can manage that, then all my scares and pain,
all my trials and tribulations would not have been in vain.
I really doubt you love me, but even if you do,
make the best decision, keep me far away from you.

You Can't Erase Me

Nonfiction by Elly Alexander, Junior
Pencil by Randi Bierly, Sophomore

You can't erase me. Like a permanent marker, I've got every intention of being here to stay. Though the end of my story could be just around the next corner, the things I do, the words I say, the legacy I leave lasts eternally. Right now, I don't just exist in this moment. I exist as a moving reel, playing over for the world to see and for the world to judge. The actions of today become the memories of tomorrow, and the memories of tomorrow become haunting reminders of the triumphs, failure and disappointments of years past. Those mistakes, those misconceptions, those rationalizations will haunt me for the rest of my life, because regret is a never ending cycle. How ironic it seems, that our mistakes follow us like shadows, while our successes are only fleeting memories.

No matter what I do, good or bad, right or wrong, the world has an opinion. Every piece of me is put on display for society to rate. I'm like stubborn graffiti on a street sign. Sure, with the right color paint you can cover me up. With the right cleaning product, you may even be able to make me go away. But like it or not, I've made my mark. Some innocent bystander driving by was influenced by my decision. My memory lives on in that bystander's subconscious. Everything I do makes a lasting impression, a chalk line body image that stays even after I'm gone. But I'm not afraid to leave. I do not fear death or change or movement. All of these come with time. They are the only constants in a transitory world. I've learned to accept my calling to move, to go. I know that I must grow and mold myself into something new, and it doesn't frighten me. Because you see, even when I've moved on and I'm way over there, at a new destination, influencing new opinions, making different choices, I'm still here, deep down in the foundation of this place. Like it or not, the world will know my name, even after I'm gone. You can't erase me.

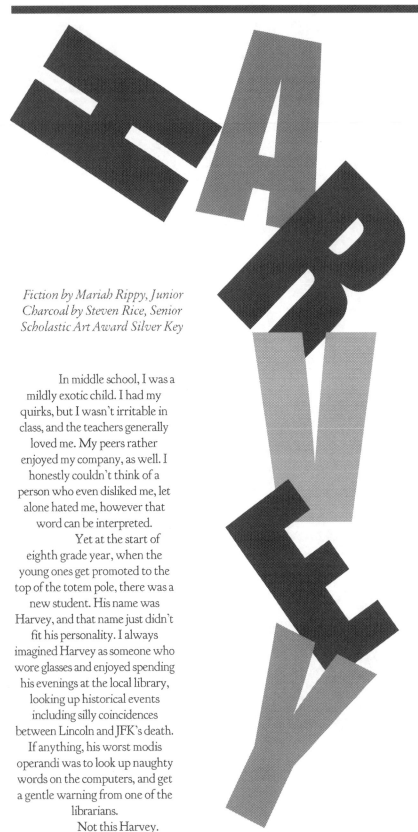

Fiction by Mariah Rippy, Junior
Charcoal by Steven Rice, Senior
Scholastic Art Award Silver Key

In middle school, I was a mildly exotic child. I had my quirks, but I wasn't irritable in class, and the teachers generally loved me. My peers rather enjoyed my company, as well. I honestly couldn't think of a person who even disliked me, let alone hated me, however that word can be interpreted.

Yet at the start of eighth grade year, when the young ones get promoted to the top of the totem pole, there was a new student. His name was Harvey, and that name just didn't fit his personality. I always imagined Harvey as someone who wore glasses and enjoyed spending his evenings at the local library, looking up historical events including silly coincidences between Lincoln and JFK's death. If anything, his worst modis operandi was to look up naughty words on the computers, and get a gentle warning from one of the librarians.

Not this Harvey.

I rarely ever rode the bus. My parents always managed to give me a car ride, especially when I complained about the bumps and noises from all the other kids. We lived close to the lake, whereas Harvey lived on the lake, and had the same route as lucky little me.

He was a large eighth grader, bright orange hair cropped neatly, along with the generic freckles spotting his face and arms. He always wore sports tees, mostly football, indicating that maybe he was on the team. He looked as if he could be. His IQ was probably well beneath average, not to mention his discipline record. I always heard whispers and rumors of him getting sent to the office multiple times for doing something in the classroom.

One morning, my mother had to work early, and my father always went into work early, whether he had to or not. I was stuck riding the smelly bus, getting up earlier than usual to meet the tall, yellow doors at the end of my long driveway. I was still only half awake as I got on, and was easy prey for the foot that suddenly stuck out to cut me down like a sapling in the woods. I tripped, with my bag flying and books falling out of my sloppily unzipped pouch. The culprit was obvious- he was howling with laughter, the result of his trip much more satisfying than he assumed it would've been. The driver noticed my fall, but didn't suspect rough-housing, considering the bus had just lurched to a start. I was a clumsy middle schooler, after all.

I struggled to help myself up. The aisle was small, and my books got trampled underneath my feet. I gathered my books as I stood, the other kids looking to the windows innocently, as if nothing had happened. Unfortunately for me, the only seat open was the one with Harvey. Nobody wanted to sit with him. I couldn't stand in the aisle forever. The driver was getting irritated, shooting glances back my way.

Taking a seat next to my new "friend," I anxiously held my bag close to my chest, sitting straight up and avoiding looking at the continuously laughing boy.

It'd been a good two minutes since the incident, and he was still tearing up with laughter. To my surprise he held a book up to me. It was my library book, one that was due that day, in fact. He grinned, reading the title out loud. I was going through a phase in middle school where I found depressing, mushy books intriguing. The titles were cheesy, and gave away the whole theme of the book in the few words.

My hand shot up to take it; he was by no means being quiet about my silly choice of reading. He snatched it away, conveniently tossing it out the half opened window in the process. At first he seemed just as shocked as me, my mouth literally dropping. But then he began to howl again, causing my eyes to tear up. I hugged my bag even tighter, the corners of my texts ⎯⎯⎯⎯⎯⎯⎯⎯⎯ But I didn't care. Just four more minutes until school. I didn't even

let myself wonder what my parents would say to the 'lost' book they would inevitably have to pay for. There was no way I was going to tell them about Harvey. I never told them about things that made me sound weak. Perhaps that's a weakness in itself. I sat with him whenever I had to get on the bus.

Fate always seemed to

have it set up that way for me. It was always full up except for the big scary boy, taking up more than the necessary amount of seat and cracking jokes about my frizzy hair.

As an adult I can see him as a taxi driver, smoking cheap cigarettes and cracking rude, ⎯⎯⎯⎯⎯⎯⎯⎯⎯⎯⎯⎯⎯ individuals who happened to pick his rusted yellow cab. The same

yellow as that bus. The smell was surely worse, probably of sweat and smoke, mixed in with fast food grease permeated into the seats. He'd probably have a growing bald spot, and be wearing those shiny cop sunglasses because he thought it was cool and ironic. There would be your typical tropical dancer, a hula skirted native on his dash, and plastic flowers as generic as his freckles hanging from the rear-view mirror.

Whatever the case, I'm happy to have him out of my hair.

We Are Writers

Poetry by Chloe Jacobson, Senior

What is a writer?
A master of chaotic frenzy
with a conscience simple
yet mastered only by man,
not driven by the will to please
but moved by the traits in which he was bred

There's the want for sustenance, for we live by bread.
and the quest to discover the right,
the grasps of love which turn us to frenzy,
the march to uncover a complicated truth within the simple
relationship of the world vs. man,
the take-no-prisoners mentality, when it comes to manners and
pleasing.

Should not a writer aim to please?
Isn't that how we, as humans, were bred?
Do not manners make the writer?
Can truth be uncovered in frenzy?
Is not the best way, also the way simple?
Is not the most intelligent also labeled man?

Or rather isn't the newest form of life also man?
When we attack, is not the first utterance by both victim and
aggressor, "please"? PLEASE!
War is fought over much less than bread;
is this truth to uncover, not a job for writers?
To make a certain sense of frenzy,
to break through the bonds of simplicity,

those knighted bonds of simplicity
which break the unwilling bonds of man?
Stories unfold where they please,
created for those starved of life as a nourishing bread.
So who is to say that manners are right?
Drama unfolds only in frenzy;

therefore Life itself is frenzy itself.
Can they not be synonyms of the same word, simply,
just as woman is a redesigned version of man?
Are not these just further projects for a writer to please?
Therefore for this, are we not bred?
Doesn't the fact that we understand this, make us all writers?

Writers are decoders of the frenzy.
The simple is the job of man to uncover.
We are born and bred to please only ourselves.

[[*Creative Sparks*]]

Slowly & Steamingly Running Through a Parking Lot

Poetry Renga by Nick Havranek, Junior;
Lina Hennig, Junior; Megan Beery,
Senior; and Danielle Wroblewski, Senior
Photo by Kate Smith, Senior

Empty parking lot,
this feels so industrial.
My emotions rot.
This feels so surreal,
Empty.

Alone is Everybody.
Some people more,
some people less.
It feels like a bad habit.
Should I break that habit?
Can I do that
alone?

Independent, it's what I thought I was,
until I opened my eyes and suddenly
everyone was gone, no one to go
home to. I pray this isn't the reality
of what it is to be
Independent.

Desolate is how things have
turned out to be.
Faces fade to darkness,
and now things are so
unreal, sitting by myself
in an empty parking lot, feeling
Desolate.

TICKING TIME BOMB

"When one burns one's bridges, what a very nice fire it makes." - Dylan Thomas
"When you set yourself on fire, people love to come and see you burn." - John Wesley

Beware the flying flashpoints of anger, pain, hate, and rage...

Double Meanings

Poetry Renga by Nick Havranek, Junior;
Kirsten Brown, Junior; Mariah Rippy, Junior;
and Chantell Cooper, Junior
Scratchboard by Morgan Tucker, Junior

Don't come back here,
your name is all I hear.
These walls, I tear.
Your eyes, they tear.

My feelings were dammed;
now we are damned.
If we still draw close,
the distance will close.

Perhaps that's a lie.
All I can do is lie
down and wait, the wind
making my mind wind.

My thoughts drift to the sea,
as other people will see
the way we lose
each other to a knot too loose.

This Is

Poetry Renga by Megan Beery, Senior;
Kelsey Mitschelen, Senior; Chloe Jacobson, Senior;
Christina Newhart, Senior; and Kassi Hall, Junior
Colored Pencil by Meredith Rogers, Junior

This is...
growing gradually, grating.
It's a fire within my heart,
threatening... threatening to overcome me.

This is...
sneaking slowly, softly.
A monster creeping up on me,
promising... promising me a broken heart.

This is...
definite, dwindling, drowsy.
It's an outcome I cannot face,
creeping... creeping closer every day.

This is...
sly, sneaky, seething.
Coming to get me,
swearing... swearing to give me pain.

This is...
falling, weird, falling.
An obstacle I can't overcome,
taking... taking me away.

Fiction by Megan Beery, Senior
Scholastic Writing Gold Key Award
Pencil by Amanda Bachtel, Senior

I'm sitting here in the kitchen, at the dining room set that he bought me for our tenth wedding anniversary. I'm hoping they will come. I didn't call them for myself; I called them for my children, Jaselle and Tina. I can handle this situation. After all, I created this problem for myself, but my daughters didn't ask for this. My sweet, innocent daughters have absolutely nothing to do with this. It's all my doing. I am Alone.

Emotion cascades down my cheeks as tears. I can hear his truck pull into the driveway. He's home early from work, which means that he'll be angry again. He might have found out about my call to the police, or he may have just had a bad day with customers, but when he's home early, the results are never good. I try to gather up my thoughts and emotions, attempting to control my tears so that I'm able to hide them from him. He hates it when I cry; I think it makes him feel bad because he knows he is the reason I cry. If he asks about the call, I decide to tell him that I didn't want to leave him, that I'll never leave him, but that I did it for the girls. I only want to protect them. I know that I cannot word it that way, though. He won't like the term "protect." He would think that I'm accusing him of being a bad father. He's never hurt them, but I don't want to give him the chance to do so. As I hear him open the front door, a chill runs up my spine. I am Afraid.

I haven't made anything for dinner yet; I must be selfish. I've forgotten to make an appointment for him; I must be stupid. I put make-up on this morning; I must be superficial. I stay quiet, hoping that his Herculean anger will not be unleashed on me. He walks into the kitchen, and perches on the edge of the table, an act either of the girls would receive a stern scolding for. He slides close to where I'm sitting, and reaches towards me. He's trying to brush the hair out of my face, but I misread his intentions and flinch away. I can see immediately the change in his manner. This is exactly what he didn't want me to do tonight, what he's not in the mood for. He sits up

[[Creative Sparks]]

straight, putting some distance between us and making his anger obvious as he crosses his arms over his chest. He tells me that I need to be more careful about the numbers that I leave on the call log. I know that he knows. I look away from him,

silently cursing my carelessness. His fist makes contact with my temple once, twice, three times. I let my forehead hit the table but I stay still. I don't want to reach up and touch the spot where he hit me. I know that showing weakness will only make him angrier. Twice he cuffs me in the side, causing my ribs to crack with a revolting crunch that makes me cringe. This hurts more

than the blows to my head, as my ribs haven't completely healed from the last time.
I am Agony.

I can hear the school bus stop outside the house, pausing briefly before it pulls away. My daughters are home, and I can only hope that he doesn't turn on them as well. They open the door, spilling into the house on a wave of laughter, school books and the autumn breeze. He leaves me where I am, slumped over the table, going out to the living room where they're standing. He gruffly tells them to be quiet, telling them that I have a headache. He's right; I do have a nasty headache. Then again, he should know; he gave it to

me. They go quietly upstairs, trying not to make a peep. They're such good girls. I thought that he would come back into the kitchen, but instead he follows them upstairs. I am Anxiety.

It's not long before I hear a crash, followed by a scream. It's Tina, my youngest daughter. She cries out again as I hear him slap her. He begins to scream at her, reminding her that I have a headache and that she must be quiet. There's a knock at the door. I expect him to stop beating Tina and come downstairs to answer the door, but he can't hear the knocking over Tina's screams. The person knocks again, so I leave my chair to answer it. I glance out the front window as I cross the living room. There's a squad car parked in the driveway behind his truck. I open the door, greeting the officer and letting him in. With so much obvious evidence, there's no room left for doubt. He comes downstairs, Tina's blood on his knuckles. When he sees the officer, he turns on me again. I close my eyes, waiting for the pain that doesn't come. The officer apprehends him, cuffs him, and takes him out to the squad car, reading him his rights as they go. I watch them pull out of the driveway before I go up to see Tina. As I climb the stairs, I am Aspiration for a better life.

DO SWEAT
the Small Stuff

Nonfiction Satire by Nathan Mauro, Senior

Pencil by Ayla Felix, Senior

Sweat, the body's way of trying to keep itself cool, is also synonymous for its foul smelling odor and uncomfortable feeling. Sweat is something most people try to avoid. With this inevitable fact in mind, one must be perplexed on the popularity of sweatpants. These, for those of you who don't know, are pants designed for you to sweat in. Yes, they are made to make you smell like an ox that just ran a marathon, look like a hobo, and kill any chance of the wearer persuading someone else that they actually care about life.

Sweatpants are often great indicators of defeat, lack of cleanliness, and lack of even enough willpower to zip and button normal pants. The primary wearers of sweatpants are high school seniors, particularly those who have developed a horrendous case of senioritis. This is mostly seen in the second semester of high school, usually after the student has already been accepted to his or her college of choice. These students even brag about the colleges they will be attending by wearing the sweatpants with the university's name and logo, to the extreme that they wear them literally every day until it's time for the sweatpant's bi-monthly wash. If colleges were smart, they would give all of their accepted students sweatpants with the institution's name on then *and then* deny acceptance to anyone actually caught wearing them in public. By following this entrance procedure, the colleges would only get the *truly* good students who really care about themselves and their academic performance.

Sweatpants are unfashionable, disgusting, and moral killers. Every pair of sweatpants on Earth should be burned in a large fire as people celebrate and dance around its unholy embers. Doing so would only make our nation a better place to live.

THINGS I
Dislike

Nonfiction by Bruce Parsons, Senior
Scratchboard by Colton Gast, Junior

There are many things I dislike, like broccoli or girls who wear wedge heels, but they are easy to explain (taste and "taste"). The things I really dislike are things that I can't explain. Things in me that make me do stupid things or make me scared of things that are seemingly harmless. It's the stuff in my mind that will not allow me to turn a homework assignment in on time. There is just something in me that says that I should not touch it until it's almost too late or is already too late.

This same distaste strikes me with applications for jobs and applying to college. I just can't make myself do it. It's like I'm scared of it. Maybe it's a fear of change or progression onward that I have had since childhood. It is always there, and when I think it's gone, it creeps up and grabs hold of me.

I dislike the little, red, beating thing in me. My heart, the thing that can be completely in love with someone and the next moment be in love with another. It can make me just so angry sometimes, because it gets to just sit there and beat away like nothing is different. I dislike the fact that my heart can control my life. That it can make me walk a direction that I would normally not even place an eye upon. That it can make me fear words that need to be said, yet make me strong enough to say some words I would never dream of saying.

I also dislike the thing in me that can make me fear the simple task of going to the principal's office. I don't know why. I just can't make myself do it unless it's a huge matter of importance. It's like the office will have the worst news possible, even though I'm just going there to ask about something small and meaningless. These things all make me wonder about myself. The funny thing about it is that I also fear the answers of why I'm like this. So it's a cycle of fear that is unfixable. These are the things I fear for their abilities to put fear in me without cause. I'm afraid that's all I can say on the matter.

Despicable Me

Poetry by Sarah Knowlton, Senior
Oil by Garrett Blad, Senior
Scholastic Art Award Gold Key

I did it again.
I thought your name.
I told you how I felt
and again,
it meant nothing.
You barely had to say a thing,
the silence and those two sentences did it all.
The silent kill.
And right then and there,
all of the emotions came flooding back
like a deadly hurricane,
a hurricane that sucked me into the depths of its violent waves.
I'm drowning in a sea of emotions.
I see flashes of the happy times, hand in hand are we,
wrapped in love, being
completely comfortable with you, then
I am smacked in the face
by a plethora of waves of sadness.
We are fighting,
crying, cheating, lying.
You are pleading for me...

Times have changed now.
I am still fighting this hurricane
in my mind,
and you are happy without me
by your side.
The tables have turned.
I am the one pleading for you,
begging for you to give me a chance,
fighting the waves, and I am drowning.
It's funny how things can change...
in a wave of an instant.

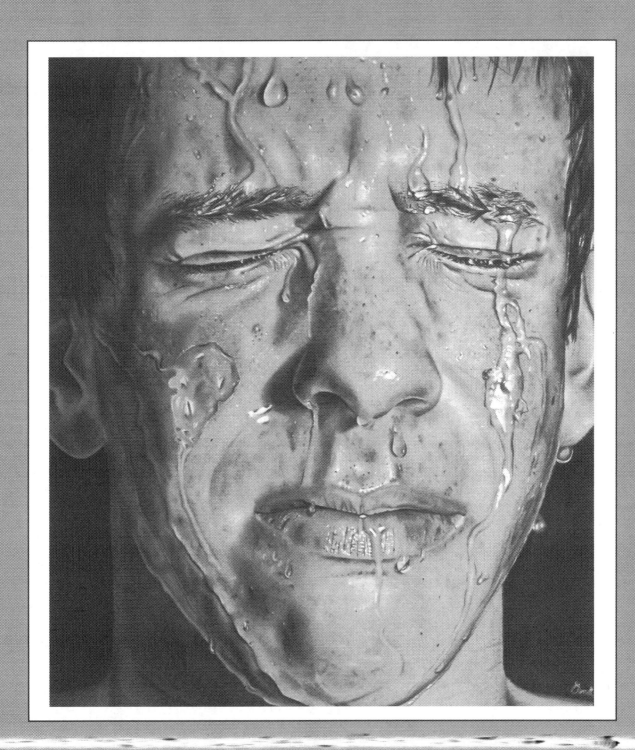

BIGBULLY

Fiction by Kirsten Brown, Junior
Scholastic Writing Award Honorable Mention
Pencil by Bree Beeney, Freshman

Absent-mindedly chewing the pink rubber on the end of my #2 pencil, I fearfully stare at the classroom door. If I avert my eyes for one second, he might sneak in when I'm off my guard. It's not long until he slowly,

menacingly sulks into the room. The dragging of his feet is like nails on a chalkboard to me. I would recognize that sound from a mile away. Even our teacher won't look him in the eye. Holding the world in his large, sweaty hands must be his only source of

entertainment. I guess when he's had years of practice, it makes sense that he won't give it up anytime soon.

He shuffles over to the desk across from my own and practically throws his books on the worn carpet. When he sits down, the stench of cologne a n d t o r t u r e fills my nostrils. Another day has begun. I think our t e a c h e r scratches numbers on the chalkboard for the first hour or so, I'm not really sure. All I can see is him. He sits there a n d scratches his arms, plays with his hair, and does anything he can to distract the rest of the class. People are nice to him because they are afraid. Sometimes I wonder if he knows that the other students don't like him. I don't think he would mind. At this point, I don't

care what kind of background he's from or why he behaves the way he does. He says he doesn't want us to accept him, and I'm fine leaving him out of everything. Unfortunately, there's always a reason for him to appear on the playground or on our journeys home.

History is the next subject, and it gets me to thinking. What will happen to this bully after school? It's obvious that college is nowhere in his future. I imagine him trapped in this town for the rest of his life, dealing with the adults that he terrified in school. It will be difficult to bully someone when you're covered in grease, checking the tire pressure on their BMW. Maybe when I come home from college I can stop by the local grocery store and have him bag my produce. There are plenty of part-time jobs around this town. I just hope he has enough talent by graduation to apply for one of them.

The ringing bell snaps me back to reality. It's already time for lunch. As everyone around me springs up from their desks, I slowly pack up my books and saunter into the hallway. My thoughts are harsh whenever I see my bully, but when he's far away, I feel sorry for him. Maybe I don't really understand his hardships. His past must have been terrible for him to act the way he does. With this thought in mind, I round the corner to the cafeteria and a large, sweaty hand smacks my books right out of my hands.

Angry Eyes

Poetry by Megan Snyder, Senior
Charcoal by Ayla Felix, Senior

My eyes felt as though
      a fistful of salt had been thrown
      into them.

All the strength of a fleet of armored tanks
      could not have stopped the deluge of
      sapphire silk as it spilled down my cherub cheeks.

Could covering my lips in a mask of duct tape
      have detained the surge of razor-tipped barbs
      as they shot out from behind my teeth?

Could I have sealed those poisonous darts in a
      lock-box and burried it somewhere in the desert,
      never to see the warm fingertips of the sun?

More importantly, could I possibly have protected
      the one light-bulb that shone out to me
      from the foggy mist?

I couldn't protect him from myself...

I settled into a sand-colored electric chair
      and let the armored tanks sink down
      in a quagmire in a state of sudden shock.

Tears glide down my cherub cheeks
      like condensation on a cold glass
      of lemonade in the summer heat.

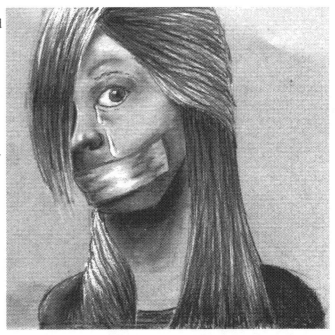

THIS is WHAT Happened.

Fiction by
Emily
Kensinger,
Senior

Scholastic
Writing Silver
Key Award

Pencil by
Nick
Havranek,
Junior

Judge if you must, but this is what I do. Everyone wants to hear how the good guy wins in the end but that's not always the case. It's never the case when you're dealing with me. There are three steps to my services: do the crime, blame the wrong guy, and get him prison time. I'm the middle man between rivals/enemies/family. I don't feel guilt or pain for what I do, and most don't agree with that. You probably won't either. One of my cases I had a few years ago will give you the best mind set of what exactly I do. He was found guilty three years ago and has twelve more years left in prison for what I made them *think* he did.

"You sure are a big fellow," said the scrawny man seated next to me at the local bar. He had yellow teeth, rancid breath and a crooked nose; he was about half my size. He was the hit.

"Not really, you're just a bit small." His background information which I spent weeks filing and collecting, made it clear he had a Napoleon Complex. This guy had been the crime boss for decades, and had a temper that made the Russian mob look like a social group you would invite over for tea and cookies. He was ruthless and very dangerous, especially when he was drinking. At that moment he was on his third beer.

His face went beet red, not from embarrassment but rage. It was pure luck that he sat down next to me. That way, I didn't have to start the scene and later have to answer questions. It was his mistake that he thought he could take me on. If only he knew. Now he does.

"Have you every tried on a pair of concrete boots?" Sam snarled through those yellow teeth, and even though I knew this man could and had done what he threatened, I needed that scene.

"No. Have you?" I patted his shoulder picking up the three strands of hair there. It shouldn't have been that easy to get, but sometimes you get lucky like that. But I still needed the blood, and as far as I know, there's no easy way around that one.

He smacked my hand away like expected and waved to his guys who started to move in. Second mistake he made.

Before he struck, his hands twitched, not into a fist that an opponent would notice, but a silent movement that would bring a hand closer to a hidden weapon, which he never carried around. He had people for that, but the memory of that silent partner never left.

It was a quick battle, broken up after a few smashed bottles, before any tables were smashed. During the tumble, I managed to withdraw the much needed blood. To this day, I still don't think he knows how I got that blood.

A couple of his goons tried going after me, but the bartender told them she had called the cops. While they tried to sweet talk her into calling them back and saying it was nothing, I made my escape and saw the cops walk into the building a minute later. They took him away for questioning, making me have to wait to do the next stage till morning.

***

Listen, you may think of my job as something the bad guys do, but I like to think of myself as one of the good guys. I use to be a cop, you know, fighting the bad guys and putting them in prison, to make this world a better place. But then you have the courts! It was ten years ago that the man walked away. He was guilty, and he got to walk after killing two kids and their mother while robbing a joint. After that I couldn't watch the bad guys slip though anymore, so I quit my job. Now the bad guys get what they deserve. Even the bad guys who hire me to deal with the competition get what's coming to them.

The guy that hired me, Toros, wanted Sam out of the picture

so he could become the top gun in town. He had been second best to Sam for so long and had tried and failed to get rid of him, causing more loss to his own men then the man he hated. I gave it two years for Sam to get comfy in his new cell and Toros to take lead of the crime in town, before I planted the evidence to get Toros the same spot as his friend Sam. Now they run the prison like they did the streets; Sam taking the lead and Toros bringing up the rear.

See, I'm not the bad guy. I get hired by a bad guy to get rid of another bad man. Once that's complete, I give it enough time so that no one would think I'm double crossing and get the first bad guy the same punishment that he made me dish out to his enemy. This way I keep getting hired by these evil, cruel, heartless men to do their dirty work, but they don't come out on top in the end. I take out so many more bad guys by doing this. It's against the law, which does upset me from time to time, but I get the bad guys away from the innocent.

One day I will be caught and won't be able to do this. They will catch me while I'm trying to get the "real" bad guy and that one will get away. But whenever that time actually comes, I will have put dozens of bad men away. It's worth the possible prison time to be able to get these men the same sentence. But let's get back to Sam.

***

He was in the jail cell for the rest of the night and part of the next day. The police knew who he was and what he did, but they didn't have enough to hold him. But once he got out, he went back to his deals, one of which would be dealing with me. I didn't know at that time that he was planning on coming after me, at least not in the way he did.

His mistake was underestimating me. After decades of being on top, Sam had started looking at everyone as a lower life form, none of whom could out smart him. But that night he came after me, which ended up working in my benefit, for I was setting the stage for "do the crime."

"So where is he?" Sam sounded pissed. He had been waiting three hours for them to catch me, but I had to finish setting the stage. Once that was done, the goons found me fast enough. It was actually impressive how fast they moved, and the bump they gave me still makes my head hurt when I think about it.

Goon Number One pulled me out of the trunk and tossed me in front of his boss. He gave me a swift kick in the stomach that looked worse than it really was. Sam wasn't that strong, and remember, he's short.

"You thought you could get away from Uncle Sam! Well, you were wrong!" Goon Number Two picked me up to stand at this point, so that Number One could sock me in the jaw. Don't let it be said I never suffered for my profession.

They thought I had given up because I wasn't fighting back, and they went to get ready to kill me. As soon as Sam and one of his Goon's left, I knocked the other goon out, right as I heard the sirens.

Tying his hands up and taking his weapons, I quickly roughed the guy up. By the time I was done with him, his shirt was torn up, he had bloody knees and a mild amount of a knockout drug I stole from Sam earlier in the week that only he used.

Sam and Number One came running back to Number Two, carrying the cement mix, to find me gone, right as the police burst into the warehouse next to the river.

They found the goods I planted fifteen minutes before and figured out his whereabouts from an "unknown caller". He was on trial for months. He got a good defense, but he was finally convicted and sent on his way to a long prison sentence. Then two years later he was joined by Toros.

I do this time and time again. There are members of the police force who know someone is out there doing this dirty work for them to get the bad guys. But they don't know who and are not in too big a hurry to find me. Forever I'll continue to get the bad guys my way, because this is the way it happens.

Monochromatic

Poetry by Megan Beery, Senior
Charcoal by Catrina Kroeger, Senior

It's all black and white;
don't try to change the lines and laws.
They shift constantly on their own.
I tried to make it right,
but there is no in-between here; flaws
find us always in the wrong with no way to atone
for words said while lost in fright.

Fright caused by this:
you're silvery blue eyes,
the gentle soothing tone of your voice,
all that I miss every time I refuse to give you a kiss.
There's the chance that you may be all lies,
that I made the wrong choice.

Choices of colors or grays,
reds or blondes, not that it changes
anything in the desires we conceal.
We've learned that less is more and subtlety pays,
so we change ourselves, we rearrange
all that we once were and we reveal,

reveal what makes us who we are:
colors muted into this gray scale,
almost all the same but unique in quiet ways.
You and I, we may live far
apart, but never doubt this, we won't fail
even though there's so much between who we are and what we say.

Say so many words of love, but
just tell me this: why am I split in two
when we fight? Give me insight for this,
please, just a bit wisdom from above
on how to make clear my view,
because I've never felt like this before.
When we're together it's so much
More than a tryst.

Trysts and flings: they don't really mean anything,
because when I close my eyes I can see what we're all about.
It's my legs and your lungs, my hair and your heartbeat.
We're one person in that moment, one being,
and among my blessings, you I never forget to count
because in my dreams, it's you I long to meet.

Meet me here, my dear.
Don't forget that you're all I need,
so just hold me as long as you want, forever
if you desire, just squeeze me until I pass out. Make clear
your love, stop my breathing, leave me broken, but I plead
just be mine all along. Make this endeavor.

Endeavor to be as we are always:
a couple with one beating heart, an affection
so plain to see that it's taken the heart of me.
We'll be like this, together, because fidelity pays
when all you'll ever want is here before you. Temptation
may tug at one earnestly, but as good as we are,
it'll never be.

It's all in colors, bright.
I've made new guides and rules;
they're finally stationary, so I'll never be alone.
I've made what's between us right.
This is where nothing is absolute; words are my tools
to express that we're all I ever wanted, all I've ever known
to be perfectly right when I go to sleep every night.

Get Thy Nails to a Nunnery!

Nonfiction Satire by Jacy Borlik, Senior
Photoshop by Amanda Bachtel, Senior

"God hath given you one face, and you paint yourselves another."
Hamlet- Act 3- Scene 1, Lines 155-156
Hamlet to Ophelia

If there is one thing in our culture that is completely unnecessary and odd, it is nail polish. It makes no sense to put a coating of colored paint on top of perfectly good nails. Not only does it reek of a strong and harmful vapor, it brainwashes our minds. Nail polish convinces us that we will be so much better looking if each one of our fingernails has a sprout of color on it. Oh, what a world of difference it would make if we all had colorful fingernails! I look around and all I see are reds and blues and greens on our hands that look so unnatural and inhuman.

Not only are these colors irradiating our fingernails, but nail polish has taken over our toenails as well! I mean, who is going to look down at our toes, anyway? People may glance at your hands (I understand that), but certainly not our feet! Why encourage foot fetish freaks?! It is all in the name of fashion. Paint is for walls and doors and cars, not for decorating our phalanges. Nail polish seems illegitimate on that part of our body. Even dogs are getting their nails painted! That is a disgrace. Nail polish is about as effective as make-up. No one really needs it, but it's slapped on anyway.

Crave, Crush, Crash

Poetry by Catrina Kroeger, Senior
Charcoal by Ayla Felix, Senior

Crave
I've developed this keen desire.
When my body aches,
She is the cure.
At times, I want her more than anything and
Can't help but to obtain her.

Sometimes
I say it's only sometimes
But it's all the time,
And I've learned that my
Addiction just cannot be quit.

Crush
This reoccurring pain never fails.
I know better, but
Knowledge alone
Can't save me from her
Or myself.

I prepare to make my futile attempt
At happiness.
Using just a photo ID, she
Crumbles under pressure
As do I.

As she looks up at me, I
Don't stop to think
That I fall for her every time.
I simply don't care.
I'm ready, surrendering.
She takes control,

Without remorse or hesitation.
She advances.
I let the substance combine with my blood,
A satisfying ratio. My eyes become
Remiss.

As the poison proceeds to penetrate my
Body, I am whole again.
Alone no longer
Truly at peace now
Take me away.

Crash
My eyes fly open like
The doors on a subway.
The tears quickly and heavily emerge,
Nothing can stop them.

She is gone again, leaving me
With that familiar craving and
Taking my happiness with her.
Emptiness comes back,
And this cycle becomes evident,
As I will be sure to
Find her again.

Forgotten Secrets

Poetry by Mariah Rippy, Senior
Scratchboard by Emily Sarber, Sophomore

Lingering smoke swells
the air and closes her throat.
Coloring pages reduce friction
between her feet and the floor,
hurling her across the den.
She'd had other things in mind for Saturday.

He was in one of his moods, Saturday.
His eyes were swelled
with tears, the forbidden
truth forever stuck in his throat.
The kitchen had new flooring.
Housework alleviated his life's fiction.

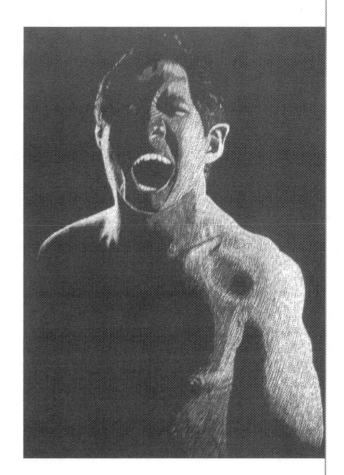

Her voice cursed with southern diction
the childrens' messes to be cleaned before Sunday.
His force slammed the door,
eyes red and swollen.
"Drinkin' again?" She cleared her throat.
"No.'Gonna panel the den."

His mind was laden
with emptiness, no benedictions
returning his memory. A cut-throat
God prevented him from church, Sunday.
The house swelled
with disappointment. He wouldn't finish the floor.

She sent him away at four.
The family was ridden
with worry; electronic ocean swells
no longer calming their addiction
to monotony. Wednesday
came around, emerging from the week's throat.

Medication slipped down his throat
as he admired the spotless tile floor.
Many Saturdays
had passed since he'd been in his den,
and he no longer recalled why his life was fiction.
Now he had a new dwelling.

She couldn't sing on Sunday; her throat was swollen.
The carpet on the floor kept friction with her rocking feet.
The den wasn't done yet; perhaps to be finished on another Saturday.

Makeup

Poetry by Brittany Tripp, Senior
Colored Pencil by Nick Havranek, Junior

Every morning I wake up feeling like I am behind bars.
This stupid crib never lets me leave when I want to.
Every day my mommy wakes me up
just so that she can take Daddy to work at 5:30 a.m.
I hate waking up that early,
and then she expects me to go right back to sleep when I get in the car!
That lady is nuts. How can I go back to sleep?
All I hear is yelling and screaming the whole way there.
When my daddy hits my mommy, he always laughs like a hyena,
but my mommy cries every time.
Why does Mommy cry?
Isn't Daddy playing with her?
He laughs because he is playing a game with her, right?
I hate to see Mommy cry
because every time she cries, Daddy gets angry.
My mommy and daddy fight a lot
because she is being too loud, so he takes her to the back room and
locks her in there.
I wonder what they do in there?
Daddy always comes out of the back room first and gets in his car and leaves.
After Daddy leaves, my mommy is still sobbing, sniveling, and sorrowing.
so I erratically walk to where Mommy is, trying not to fall on my way there.
When I enter the room, Mommy sees me and wipes her tears,
then picks me up and begins to cry again.
I don't understand what is wrong. Why is she crying?
Mommy had a new style of makeup on today though.
 I don't know why Mommy would ever change her makeup;
 her kind red lips and sparkling blue eyes make her look so beautiful.
Mommy has her red lipstick on but it seems to be running
down the side of her face,
and her eyes are not as radiant today.
She has a kind of purple eye makeup on around her whole eye.
I bet that's why Daddy took Mommy in the back room;
he just wanted to help her with her makeup!
I have to say, Daddy cannot put makeup on like Mommy can.

my STORY

Nonfiction by Danielle Wroblewski, Senior
Scholastic Writing Silver Key Award
Photo by Danielle Wroblewski, Senior
Photo by Jessiva Figueroa, Senior

I knew as soon as I'd exceeded the amount of oxycodone my body could handle that things would never be the same. In my last few moments of awareness, the previous few months became like a slide show before my eyes. I was able to see all the things that had led me to that point. I pulled my blanket of chemical comfort closer to soak in warmth when my body started to shake.

While my system fought half of a bottle of pills, my mind was in slow motion. A few memories in particular made me realize, in that moment, I didn't regret making that choice. I couldn't bring myself to regret something that offered to save me from the constant memories that had me hiding in the darkness, rather than running from it. The first memory sent another jolt down my spine, moving me harder against the cold wooden floorboards.

I've never really realized that best friends don't make good lovers. I'm brought back to my freshman year, and it's spring. The weather is wet and cold, but a warm breeze reassures us that better temperatures will be coming soon. His hand is wrapped around mine, the skin of his palm calloused but gentle to the touch. His eyes are a clear blue, a reflection of the sky that hung above us. We are young, and our hormones make us believe that we are in love.

Looking back, we may have realized that it was purely just a hormonal reaction to each other, but at the time, I was convinced that he was the illusive "one." When I thought about my future, I always saw him right there with me. Tyler always made me feel like I was the most important thing to him. I may have thought that I had fallen for him, but I was too young to completely give myself to him. I realize now that that was the reason he left. Tyler was the kind of guy who was only going to be around long enough to gain what he could, but after that, he'd disappear from your life and be nothing but a ghost from your past. He left my life in April. Tyler was the beginning of many months of hardships, and June came too soon after.

June 8, 2008. That date ceases to exist on any calendar that I own. Instead, it is whited out with "No, no, no, no," written in every free inch of that conforming square. That day was hot, summer burning in the air with mango smoothies and charcoal-colored clouds. A storm was approaching, and he had a thunderbolt in his thoughts. He knew exactly what to do. After the "incident" (as the courts refer to it), it started to rain. When the only pure thing that I had left was stolen from me, the sky started to cry with me. I knew that after that day, I was altered, the old me left in dark closet spaces.

My recollections continue, going over the following months like a horror film. Night terrors, emotional warfare, and physical disgust. I remember not being able to look at myself in the mirror without wincing and my stomach knotting up. I found a rebound to help me forget about my experience, but he was only fuel to the flame. His name was Matt.

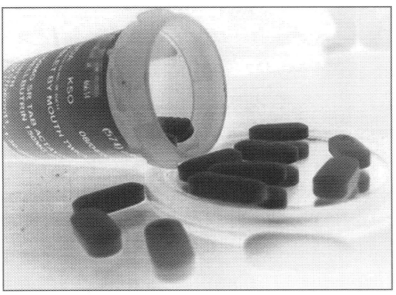

Back then, there was a social gathering where I went every Tuesday. It was called drum circle, and I always went with my best friends. The day that I met Matt there should have never happened. I wish that it hadn't. Still recovering emotionally, I trusted him too easily and believed him when he said that he would care for me. Matt was July. July was filled with tell-tale bruises and screaming. I still hear our fights playback in my mind like a recording on replay. I spent the night in a hospital bed the last time he raised his hand to me. No lasting damage, the doctor said. He didn't mean emotional, obviously. Those scars will last a lifetime. Lesson learned.   School was going to start soon, and I knew it wouldn't be the same as before. I was different. The way I saw everything was different, too.

My sophomore year at Washington High School started, but I shut everything out. A month later, brown eyes consumed me. I'm not quite sure he came into my life, only that he became everything to me. He had a rough tone to his voice

and a wicked sense of humor, but he completed me in a way that I never expected to happen. My thoughts of Tyler disappeared soon, and Nathan became the only thing I saw somehow. I jump to a different memory now.

Friendly and familiar faces all looking expectantly towards me is what I see next. I feel all the things I felt that day again, each emotion and twist in my gut reminds me even more vividly of my 16th birthday. I knew my family was waiting for me to do something, to do anything, but I was still frozen in place with my systems still in shock from news that I had received just moments before. I felt my best friend Melanie touch my arm gently and ask me if I was okay, but I couldn't register the question enough to make a motion towards the proper answer of "No."

See, cell phones are a funny thing. They can show other people things that the owner may not have actually intended to become common knowledge. A person can simply get reckless and forget to erase one small thing, and without knowing it, that little thing makes all the difference.

My boyfriend should have thought about that at the time.

In one instant, because of his carelessness, I knew that he had lied to me all along. I knew who she was before he even told me. Maybe, I had known all along but never accepted it before I had to. Or maybe, he never really was mine to begin with. I looked at him and whispered, "Why? Why did you do it?" His only answer was to close his eyes and shrug. He couldn't even explain to me why he had cheated on me. Soon enough, my inferiority complex kicked in and my mind shut down, again.

"No, no, no, no," were the last words that I said to him that night before I walked out.

At this point in my life, being lost was kind of a beautiful thing. Being broken was beautiful to me. Everyone knew not to expect too much or hope for too much because it was already assumed that I would just let them down. They would only be disappointed. I spent that fall walking in the woods and watching the leaves turn to shades of amber and crimson before they fell to the ground. On the ground they were rendered a vapid, lifeless brown.

Halloween came abruptly, and somewhere along the way, I had made many new friends. Little white pills were my best friends, keep-sakes from my father's medicine bottles. I loaded my body with medication and decided to celebrate Halloween with my real-life friends Ariel, Melanie, Ashley, and Corie. We were all flawed in our own ways. The five of us were parts of a working system that we called a family even though none of us were actually related. We told each other almost everything but trusted no one, not even ourselves. We dressed up in costumes as the night filled with each of our own personal drugs of choice. My pills stayed close by my side.

Much of that Halloween is vague to me. I remember bright, colorful lights flashing around us and music loudly filling the room we were in. It was a rave, and everywhere you turned, there were bodies pulsing to the beat that engulfed your body as soon as you walked in. It was a sensory overload. We stayed there for a little while and decided to take a try at trick-or-treating next. I'm not sure where we started or even ended up; I just remember the relief that I felt as soon as we were back at Ariel's house, reeling from our wild night. We turned on a cd of Rob Zombie, and each of us mellowed out to our own tunes within the songs. The next thing we knew, the sun was rising, and our bloodshot eyes and dilated pupils hid nothing from wondering eyes. Sleep had evaded us the past night, and we spent the day recovering and recollecting the events of the previous 24 hours, stopping routinely to laugh about what each of us remembered.

By Thanksgiving, I'd stopped looking for meaning in anything that happened. Days mixed together in a blur of sound and color. I'd lost my smile and felt hollow inside, but somehow I knew that I was still there. At least, some part of me was. My next friend was marijuana. My little white and round friends from before became a side to my group. The only downfalls of weed were that they made me sleepy and want to eat a lot, but I didn't want to sleep. I saw things and heard voices when I slept. To fix that problem, I added Adderall to the equation. Adderall kept me from sleeping when I didn't want to and it kept me feeling calm and in control. You'd be amazed what you can get

accomplished without eight hours wasted each night, or fifty-six hours wasted each week.

I was growing progressively, my knowledge of drugs expanding everyday. I tried ecstasy, which is otherwise known as ''E,'' ''X,'' ''Thizz,'' or ''XTC''. Acid was next, followed soon by heroin and crystal meth. I only tried those last two drugs once. I wasn't looking for an addiction, just a cure. However, cocaine was a different story entirely. When you snort, you need to watch your amounts and not get careless. There's a thin line between too much or too little, and you had to know how much you could handle. It was like a jolt of lightening to my brain. The second the sweet white powder hit my system, any chaos in my mind stopped instantly. I was floating above everything, and I became a newer, more improved me. I lived like this for a while, until one mishap turned everything upside down.

Sometimes, when people see that you're too happy, they get jealous and ruin it for you. The problem is, you can never trust anybody. That's what happened to me. Her name was Stephanie. She had known me for a long time and saw that what I was doing to myself by taking drugs was unhealthy. Stephanie got ''concerned'' and told my parents everything. Until then, I had done a pretty good job at hiding my actions outside of my home. My parents decided that in order to really find out if she was right, they had to drug test me. For me, that didn't go so well.

For a while, I figured that I would play along with the ''system.'' I stopped doing drugs, or so everyone else thought. I resorted to a new venue, a more widely domesticated and abused drug:

alcohol. I tried every drink that I could get my hands on. My parents said that I couldn't do drugs anymore, but they didn't refer to alcohol. It was easier to get and not as difficult to conceal from the people who watched me. The best part was that I wouldn't test positive for it on routine drug tests.

At this point in my memory, it was just past Christmas. Not quite New Year's yet, but that time in between the two holidays. I was always medicated, which was my new, creative substitution term for ''intoxicated.'' I was lying in bed with my bedroom window open so I could feel the fresh, icy wind that winter always seems to produce, but I wasn't cold. The alcohol in my system was like fire in my veins.

My memory continues on like this, an endless strand of connecting events. I snap back to reality like an elastic band breaking, and I'm still shaking on the floor with the ticking clock by my side, which grimly reminds me that only a few minutes have actually passed, though it has felt like hours. Even now I can find some humor in how things can only take seconds to remember, but it'll take hours or even days to actually live them. Or to survive them, if you do. Not everybody does. We all have an expiration date eventually.

I feel my pulse slow significantly, and my breathing feels somehow hollow and less satisfying, like my body itself is suffocating and the air that I am trying to get isn't doing anything for me. I see things more softly now, their edges and definition fuzzy and bright. I smile and sigh quietly, ready for what I expect to come next, until I hear footsteps outside the bedroom doorway. My heart starts to race beneath the weight of the oxycodone. Instantly, I want to run or hide but my body is frozen in place by some delayed shock.

The door opens, and I strain to see the face of my best friend, Melanie, but my eyesight is too weak and everything becomes broken down into fractals, each one losing their clarity. I fight to rush to the dark wave of chemical compounds that are lapping at my awareness. I want to escape from this vague sense of disappointment. The last sound that I hear among the persistent 'tick tick tick' of my alarm clock is Melanie's voice screaming, "Danielle, no, no, no, no!" I see her crystal clear blue eyes watering over me. I see black next.

Waiting, waiting, blackness.

In what seems like the blink of an eye, I'm awake. My chest aches, my throat burns, and my entire body is throbbing. Apparently, getting your stomach pumped has a lot of drawbacks. Waking up is always the hardest part. I know that I didn't accomplish my goal. I failed. I never thought to factor in certain points about my plan. I didn't think about how Melanie's parents were trained paramedics and that they weren't on call that day. I didn't think any of that all the way through. My last memory of that day before my recovery was a man's gentle but firm voice. For the first time since the "incident," someone thought to ask me something meaningful. He simply asked, "Danielle, are you with us?"

Delayed but also firm, my answer eventually was, "Yes."

After I recovered physically, I had to regain many of my emotions back. I could feel them hiding within me, somewhere deep beneath the surface, but I didn't know how to find them. Seeing the

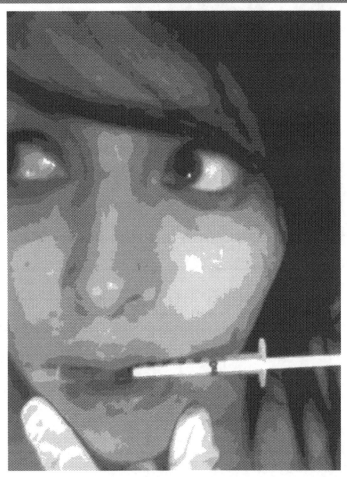

faces of my friends and family the day I woke up in the hospital after the attempt to end my life made me realize where I had found myself in life. By choosing a dead-end path, I had hurt many of the people I cared about. I realized and I wished that I had gotten help sooner, so I decided to get sober once and for all on my own. I landed myself in this position to begin with, and I knew that I had to be the one to get myself out of it.

I discovered the hard way that after you overdose, you tend to have a few problems with your senses after that. From my attempt, I lost much of my ability to hear, and my eyesight never fully recovered. Some of my taste buds disappeared and my sense of touch hasn't seemed quite as specific since then. Staying

sober is always the hardest part, though. I think that once you make drugs such a high priority in your life and become addicted to a certain point that even after you quit them, there's always still part of you that will want a fix.

I know that forever, or for as long as I can imagine, part of my mind will always be screaming to just pop one pill or just take one hit because it couldn't possibly hurt. It can only make me feel better. I'll want that one drink, too. It will be a constant internal fight to stay clean because once you've had a taste of any of those crutches, you'll always be hooked to some degree.

This blessing in disguise, will forever now be my curse in plain sight.

Nonfiction by Olivia Hurley, Senior

Photo by Kate Smith, Senior

'm usually a very nice person. I don't complain or throw around my opinions. I kind of have a title as "the nice girl." That ticks me off, though; I'm no nicer than anyone else. I'm upfront with people and tell them how it is, but yet everyone still sees me as a shy, quiet girl. Look deeper.

For your information, here are a few things that really get me started: girls who take absolutely forever in the bathroom; there are four stalls in there! Seriously, how can four girls stay in there for the same length of time? Are they waiting for someone to flush first? Or when I get done and I go to wash my hands, there are girls standing there in front of the mirror putting on makeup or fixing their hair. That's only half of what ticks me off.

I don't like it when my friend talks like she's from downtown South Bend: "She be talkin to me like 'dis, act'n like she all hood" or she'll be calling me "dude." She also says the word "bet" a lot. What is that supposed to mean? What am I "betting" on? Supposedly, "bet" means you're happy about something; for example, your mother tells you she's getting you an iPod, and you would say, "BET." Don't talk to me unless you learn to speak proper, first grade English.

I hate people who make fun of my height. Hello, I realize I'm like 4 foot nothing, but do you have to throw your two cents in there. I don't think so.

I also hate parents that let their 13 year old daughters dress like skanks and then let them date 20 year old men. I think a few people need a smack of reality. I hate all the Disney channel characters who think they are able to sing. More than half of them aren't even good, but they still go on tours and release albums. They're brain washing little kids with horrible music.

I hate when people constantly ask me what's wrong. If something is wrong, I'll tell you, but for now leave me alone.

I hate when people use words like "stupidest," "acrossed," or "bob-wire" (barbed-wire). They are not words and are not correct. You learn this every year in Language Arts. It is "most stupid," or you replace it with a word such as "dumbest." You can ask your Language Arts teacher or an intelligent parent. What a stupid grammar mistake to make!

I also hate girls! I can't stand them. And I'm a girl! I've noticed that all the girls around me are filled with drama, looking for anyone to pick a fight with. Then you'll mention something you don't like (a certain sport or type of music), and UH-OH, World War III has broken out, because they get all defensive over some stupid thing. Grow up. You make yourself look pathetic.

I hate when people yell at games on the television. Yelling, "COME ON" or "YOU IDIOT" isn't going to help you or them do any better. Knock, knock, the people in the TV can not hear you.

I also hate people who hate too much. I'm almost surprised I don't hate myself. Don't worry, that isn't going to stop me because my list could go on and on...

Flowers

Poetry by Ayla Felix, Senior
Scholastic Writing Award Honorable Mention
Colored Pencil by Garrett Blad, Senior
Scholastic Art Award Silver Key

The vase sits in the middle of the table,
with its drooping flowers and murky water.
The heavy scent of dying flora fills the air.
It makes me think of a funeral. It might as well be.
The card says ""Happy Anniversary," but
it's not happy. Not at all.
And the decaying flowers just add to that unhappiness.
A cold breeze rushes in as the door is opened;
I look and it's only you.
"Hey, honey," you say,
as if I don't know.
As if everything is okay.
Nothing's "okay" anymore.
"Hey, I like the flowers."
I lie, and you grin.
"I'm glad. I just stopped to pick up a few things;
I have to catch my flight in a few hours."
I nod. You go up to our bedroom
and I can hear you moving around; I don't follow.
Sometime later, who knows how long,
you come downstairs and hug me briefly.
Then you're gone.
"I know about her," I tell the vase
with its drooping roses and sad looking lilies.
They don't answer me.
The sound of breaking glass and dripping water
is oddly unsatisfying.

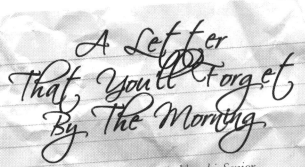

A Letter That You'll Forget By The Morning

Nonfiction by Danielle Wroblewski, Senior

I stopped eating because I was already empty. There was already a hole in my torso that wasn't going away. It wasn't going to heal and I wasn't going to be okay. I wanted to be perfect. Just for you, I was trying to be perfect. To be everything you ever wanted. I wanted to love myself; to play beautiful melodies on my cracked rib cage and believe that nobody ever dies.

I took pills to feel something. To feel anything that wouldn't remind me of you. I took as many as I could as quickly as I could to block out the thoughts of you that were constantly in my head. Vicodin was to forget your touch. Oxycontin was to forget your voice. Ecstasy was to forget the way you looked at me, like I actually mattered for once. Adderal was to escape the dreams that turned into nightmares when you walked out on me.

I drank to feel a burning in my throat, and not in my eyes. The fifth's of Vodka and shots of Jack made me feel pretty, even if it was only while my head was spinning. Some nights, I felt that maybe if I drank more, I'd be so pretty that maybe you would come back and wouldn't walk away, again. After all the alcohol was gone, I think that's when I realized I really was alone, and that you were never coming back.

I inhaled smoke to feel weightless. I felt that if I smoked everything I could find that could make me float, then maybe all the fractured broken pieces that are left of me wouldn't have to be on the ground anymore. I was tired of being on the ground and not being able to get up on my own.

I snorted for release. To give in and give up my control. To be happy, without depending on you to make me smile. I only blushed when I felt the rush of white powder hit my system and the room disappear, even for only moments. For moments, I was invincible.

I wrote this to tell you; I'm messed up. I've been used and thrown away. I still cry, and I'm still broken. I don't know who I am, but I know what I am. I'm a disaster, and you made me this way. I still love you, and I'll still have some of these habits as long as I love you. It's the only way to live without you that I know.

Love, Me.

Monsters Are Only Supposed To Exist In Fiction

Poetry by Danielle Wroblewski, Senior
Photo by Danielle Wroblewski, Senior

Broken things are beautiful;
you'd think once I realized that,
I'd consider myself beautiful, but I still don't.

I don't know how I got here, but I woke up on this cold wood floor,
feeling the stinging it caused against my burning skin.
I counted the pieces of me to see how many had shattered
this time. I can't remember exactly when I lost count,
but I felt that the number exceeded the standards set
by the word "broken," if there were any at that point.

I could feel the fire slithering from my veins,
slowly inviting the frost in to sleep
between the cracks of my shield, adding more along with them.
I wonder if he'll ever miss the sparkle in my eyes or
the gentle flush my cheeks developed when he made me laugh,
because they're not here anymore, either.

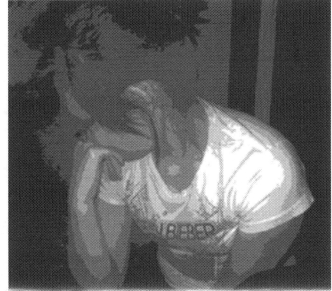

I could hear the steady rhythm of my heart
beating in every part of my body and
realized that he didn't physically have my heart,
but instead he was the only reason
it was even put there to begin with.

Monsters are only meant to exist in fiction.

    Right?

THE LAST NIGHT

Drama by Megan Beery, Senior
Scholastic Writing Silver Key for Science Fiction/Fantasy
Pencil by Cheyenne McLachlan, Senior

Narue is standing in a meadow full of fluttering blue and black butterflies. She's standing alone, waiting, searching for something intently. The trees part, and Night Owl steps out of the shadows into the starlight. He begins to walk toward Narue, disrupting the thousands of butterflies as he makes his way to her.

Narue: Don't, Owl. You'll disturb them.

Night Owl: Disturb who? We're alone.

Narue: The butterflies, don't hurt them, Owl.

Night Owl: I'm not hurting them. *He stops walking anyway, afraid to get too close to her. She might run away again.*

Narue: I've missed you. I was wondering when you'd come back to see me.

Night Owl: I had to track down some of the others. I didn't mean to be gone for so long.

Narue: Are they …

Night Owl: They weren't in any pain. I doubt if they even knew what was happening to them,

Narue: They knew.

Night Owl: I know. *A weight seems to settle on his shoulders as he finally admits this to himself.*

Narue: This is wrong. I'm not a "thing"; none of us are.

Night Owl: I know, but none of you are normal either. You're dangerous to the rest of us.

Narue: I'm dangerous? Are you afraid of me? *She looks at him intently, her pupil-less blue eyes searching for more than simply his answer*

Night Owl: No, I'm not and neither are you. I mean (*he begins to massage his temples with his fingertips*) Damn, do you know how hard this is for me? Another hunter could catch you, and I would have no idea until it was too late. My commander could find out that I've been letting you go and then I'd be…

Narue: I'm sorry.

Night Owl: I check the lists of the apprehended every time I'm in camp, searching for the assurance that you're still out here. That you're still all right.

Narue: *Appearing suddenly at Night Owl's side and gently touching his shoulder.* Don't worry, we're fine, Owl. We'll always be fine. No other hunter could find me, much less catch me. This is my home. I grew up here, and I know it better than anyone else ever could.

Night Owl: But they're designing new hunters. Specialized men who're taught to find your kind and kill them. They're more than hunters. My commander calls them 'trackers' and he wants me to become one. He thinks that I've got what it takes to survive the training.

Narue: They've trained hunters to find us before, and we're still here. We'll get through this, too.

Night Owl: These men will be different. Like you, they won't be human anymore.

Narue: I'm still human

Night Owl: No, you're not. You look human and mostly you act like it, too, but you're more. You can

〚 Creative Sparks 〛

move so quickly no hunter can see how quickly you move. And your eyes, they're, well, they're—

Narue: My eyes allow me to see. You think that I asked to be this way? That as a normal, happy child I just had to be different and I decided to change? I didn't ask for terrorists to drop a nuke on my town or for them to kill my family. I didn't ask for all of my friends to disappear in the blink of an eye or for my country to suddenly decide that I'm a monster.

Night Owl: I didn't mean it that way; I don't think that you're a monster.

Narue: No, of course not. You just kill people like me.

Night Owl: You know why I became a hunter. It had nothing to do with you. Hell, I didn't even know you when one of your kind killed Nanome. I didn't know that not all of you were violent.

Narue: I know that you did it for your sister, but now I'm asking you to quit. For me. *She cups his jaw in her hand and turns his face to look at her.*

Night Owl: I can't. My commander will know that I'm gone and then they'll track me. *He touches the bump on his left bicep, where a circular bulge protrudes. His tracking device begins to warm up with contact.*

Narue: I could make your commander disappear, if you asked me to.

Night Owl: They'd kill you, Narue.

Narue: But then you'd be free.

Night Owl: Nothing is worth your life. You're precious.

Narue: *She leaves his side, reappearing across the meadow,*

butterflies landing on her hair and shoulders. I love you, Owl.

Night Owl: I love you too, my Narue.

Narue: I have to go now.

Night Owl: Don't leave yet. *He makes his way across the meadow's gently swaying grasses while Narue waits for him.*

Narue: Don't be away for so long this time. I miss you whenever we're not together.

Night Owl: You'll hardly even know that I was gone. *He wraps his arms around Narue and presses his lips to hers.*

Narue: Someday I'll make it all go away. When you're ready, I'll make this disappear. *She touches his*

tracking device with her fingertips briefly.

Night Owl gives her one last kiss and holds her close before they part ways. Narue disappears, returning to her hideaway in the forest, and Night Owl goes back to the city and his occupation as a hunter for the US military.

Commander: Are you ready to complete the training?

Night Owl: Yes, sir.

Commander: Are you dedicated to this program?

Night Owl: Yes, sir.

Commander: (*To doctor*) Give him the last round of radiation. Do it right this time, don't ruin him. I want him to be perfect.

Doctor: That was a fluke .

Commander: It almost cost me a damn good hunter. Now, make him a tracker.

The doctor slides his mask over his nose and mouth before initiating the machine.

The commander steps behind a lead wall and goes into an observation room. He nods silently before the Doctor begins.

Doctor: This may hurt a bit more than your previous treatments. This is the final dose and it will change your eyes, the way that you see.

Night Owl: *(He shifts apprehensively within his restraints.)* This is what I want. Just do it.

Doctor nods silently and flips a switch on the machine.

Night Owl begins to tense, his muscles flexing against the pain. He groans and starts to sweat; the effects of the treatment are starting to get to him. He bites back a scream and his eyes roll back as he is unable to contain another. The doctor turns up the levels of radiation as the commander watches, a sadistic smile pulling at his lips. Night Owl closes his eyes and loses consciousness to the sound of his own screams. When he begins consciously thinking again, he realizes that he's standing in the training field with his commander and a muscular man about his own age. The open air feels good against his skin. It's complete freedom in comparison to the surgical room, with its low light and padded beds with leather restraint straps.

Commander: Both of you boys have done me proud. You've gone above and beyond the call of duty to protect your country and your families. These creatures are vile and cunning, so never underestimate them.

Especially the first generations. They were created during the initial attack on the homeland, and they were infected by the enemy's influence first. The ones that are still left out there have survived for a good reason. Believe me when I say that they are what you were created to fight – and destroy. You two are brothers now, nothing comes between you. Am I clear?

Night Owl: Yes, sir.

Wolfbane: Hoorah!

Commander: There's a pair of first generations west of here, and I want you boys to bring 'em back here, dead or alive. Now get a move on.

Both trackers run west, and the commander watches them go, esteem evident in his posture. The trackers run until they enter a forest. Going within the darkness of the trees, they continue past sundown and eventually they reach a meadow with long, flowing grass.

Wolfbane: Were we supposed to come to this place, brother?

Night Owl: I think that they're here. This place reeks of their stench. *His white, pupil – less eyes look over the meadow as butterflies land on his automatic weapon and over his shoulders.*

Wolfbane: Ever been here before?

Night Owl: No, not that I remember.

Walfbane: That's the worst part of it, ain't it? All that you lose, like it never even happened.

Night Owl: *Shakes his gun to scare the butterflies off of it.* Yeah.

Wolfbane: I wonder why all these bugs are here. It must be their mating season, huh? *He wiggles his eyebrows expressively.*

Night Owl: No, they live here all the time.

Wolfbane: What? I thought that

you hadn't been here before.

Night Owl: It's just one of those feelings. The ones that I almost... almost remember.

Wolfbane: Just not all the way, right?

Night Owl: Yeah, it's really nagging at me.

Wolfbane: I hate those. They drive me nuts.

Night Owl: Me too, brother. There's nothing here, Let's keep moving.

Wolfbane: Nothing but butterflies. *He watches as Night Owl begins to head north, towards the closest section of the forest. West is this way. See something over there?*

Night Owl: I thought I did. It's nothing.

Narue: *(Appears before the two trackers, with a tall, willowy brunette standing next to her.)* Owl! It's been nearly ten months; I thought that you'd forgotten about me. I've been so worried –

Wolfbane: It's them! *He opens fire on the two women and kills the woman who was with Narue.*

Narue: *(She disappears, reappearing instantaneously behind Night Owl).* Owl, who is he?! He killed Teresa. Why did you let him do that? *Night Owl spins around, pressing the barrel of his weapon again Narue's sternum.*

Wolfbane: *(Trains his sights on Narue.)* Do you know her, brother?

Narue: *(Looks at Night Owl and notices that his eyes have changed. Gone are his silvery irises, all that's left is the white eye.)* You're not my Owl. You're a monster!

Wolfbane: What's it talking about, Night Owl?

Night Owl: *(Falters as he stares into Narue's blue eyes.)* I'm not a monster.

Narue: I never wanted you to do

Digital Art by Cheyenne McLachlan, Senior

this. *She disappears, reappearing momentarily to pick up Teresa's body before running towards the woods.*

Wolfbane: (*Drops all of his gear to be able to run faster, beginning to chase Narue.*) She'll be slower while she's carrying the other one!

Night Owl: Beat you there?

Wolfbane: Hoorah!

Night Owl runs after Narue, quickly passing Wolfbane and leaving him behind. When he catches up with Narue, he pushed her against a tree, knocking Teresa from her arms in the processes.

Narue: (*Glares up at her captor.*) Monster.

Night Owl: I'm not a monster. *He releases her and turns away to look at Teresa's body, which is lying at an odd angle.*

Narue: I never truly believed that you were. Let me make it disappear, Owl.

Night Owl: (*Turns sharply to look at her, his face instantly softening.*) I... I remember you. You're Narue.

Narue: (*Rushes up to him and wraps her arms around his torso.*) Why did you do it anyway, even after I told you not to?

Night Owl: I wanted to know what it was like.

Narue: What what was like?

Night Owl: What it's like to be you.

Narue: (*Tugs at his hand, pulling him deeper into the forest as Wolfbane approaches.*) Well, now you know.

Night Owl: Yeah, now I know.

Narue: How does it feel?

Night Owl: Absolutely Amazing, but horrible at the same time. I'm sorry about Teresa.

Narue: We'll come back for her.

Night Owl: I meant I'm sorry that she's –

Narue: I know what you meant.

Night Owl: Narue?

Narue: What, Owl?

Night Owl: Can you make it disappear?

Narue: Yes. *She leads him behind a tree and reaches into her right boot. Pulling out a knife, she cuts into his left bicep. Slicing it open and reaching into the gash, she pulls out the little metal tracking device. She quickly drops it on the ground as it has grown incredibly hot, to try and prevent anyone from touching it. She crushes it under her boot before wiping her knife off in the grass and replacing it in her boot.*

Night Owl: Alright. Let's keep going. *He uses his right hand to squeeze his left bicep to help slow the bleeding.*

Narue steps out from behind the tree to continue their escape.

Wolfbane: Stop, not another step. Where is he? What did you do to him?

Night Owl: I'm fine, brother. *Follows Narue out, pushing her behind himself protectively.*

Wolfbane: But your tracking device. The monitor said that it stopped registering your heart rate. You should be dead now. *His stares at Night Owl's bloody arm as understanding dawns over his features. He's holding a thin, hand held computer that monitors the tracking devices.*

Night Owl: Don't worry about it. Take the other one back to Commander. I'll get this one.

Wolfbane: See you soon. *He salutes Night Owl.*

Night Owl returns the salute. Wolfbane disappears into the underbrush.

Narue: Owl, is he really your brother?

Night Owl: No, he's just another tracker.

Narue: He's a tracker? But his eyes weren't right. They were normal.

Night Owl: The doctor didn't radiate him correctly, and they had to halt his training. He's got the speed, but his eyes can't keep up, which is why he's slower than you and I.

Narue: (*Cuddles against Night Owl's chest.*) I love you, Owl. Please don't leave again. I can't live here alone, without Teresa. I'll go crazy.

Night Owl: Hush. Don't say things like that. I'll stay with you, I promise. *He closes his eyes and rests his cheek on top of her head.* I love you, too.

Narue gasps suddenly and becomes stiff, her eyes wide in surprise, pain searing through her back.

Wolfbane: I knew that something was wrong with you, brother. The moment you hesitated to pull the trigger on her, I knew. She was what you almost remembered, right? Well, remember her like this. *Twists his knife deeper into her back before pulling it out.*

Narue cringes and falls to the ground as Night Owl lunges at Wolfbane, pinning him up against a tree.

Night Owl: I hope that your eyes can keep up, brother, because you're going to have one hell of a time

trying to see me. *He disappears, letting Wolfbane slide to the forest floor.*

Wolfbane: You couldn't have stayed with her. She's just a creature, remember? She's not even human.

Night Owl: You think you're human? We're nothing but damn machines! Look at what we've done to ourselves! We've twisted the very meaning of what it is to be human. You think that we're so great, that

---

> **❝** You think you're human? We're **nothing but damn machines!** Look at what we've done to ourselves! We've twisted the very meaning of what it is to be human. **❞**

---

we're such great people. You look up to me, but you're worshiping a machine. *His voice is faraway. It sounds as if it's coming from above Wolfbane's head.*

Wolfbane: Don't be ridiculous. You've fallen right into her tricks. She deserved to die; we were created to protect humans from things like her.

Night Owl leaps down from his perch in a tree above an unsuspecting Wolfbane. He lands a right hook to Wolfbane's jaw and the two begin to wrestle. Wolfbane

tries to utilize his advantage of having a weapon, but he can't seem to get a good angle on Night Owl, as he can't see him very well. Night Owl is moving with the speed of a tracker, and Wolfbane's eyes can't register his movements as anything more than blurs. Night Owl slows momentarily, taking a breath and flicking away the trickles of blood left by Wolfbane's various small slashes in his skin. Wolfbane takes his chance and drives his knife into Night Owl's stomach. Wolfbane struggles to his feet, bruised and bleeding from his tussle with Night Owl. He backs away from the man he once called brother, from the man he once looked up to and leans against a nearby tree to watch him die.*

Wolfbane: Do you want to be cremated, like all the great warriors?

Night Owl: No, bury me with her.

Wolfbane: Even now, when I give you the chance at redemption for the next life, you choose to stay with her, with a tainted creature?

Night Owl: *Taking his final breath, he murmurs his last words.* You're wrong. She was more human than either you or I. She didn't choose this life; she was content to be what she was. But we weren't, and we forced ourselves to be what we were never meant to be.

My Nemesis

Poetry by Megan Snyder, Senior
Charcoal by Ayla Felix, Senior

I rage at the cerulean sky,
    shaking my mangled fist at
    the empty expanse of blue above me.
My eyes slide to the cobalt depths
    in which a horrible beast scared me
    into a white fear that swallowed me whole.
I hate him with a fire that can not be stamped out
    nor watered down by a cool rain.
He will pay for what he has done to me,
    what causes me such pain every time I reach up
    to touch my chin or straighten my hat.
"He'll crow. He'll fight. And then... he'll die."

The words I swore on the day he took my hand,
    I swear again as I harangue towards the silver clouds
    that I feel will, so soon, open up and allow
    my long-nines to clear a wide hole in his prideful chest.
A whistle sounds under a foot of deck timber.
    What idiot has broken my menacing reverie?
    Men begin shouting around me, squawking like the
    birds that lazily float around the ship, pointing up at the
    sky with grubby fingers, at a slim silhouette gliding round
    the main mast and rigging.
"Take him down! Shoot him!"

I scream at the soaring shape, trying to bring it down with the sound of my voice.
I shake my mangled fist at him and yell,
"I'll get you Peter Pan if it's the last thing I do!"

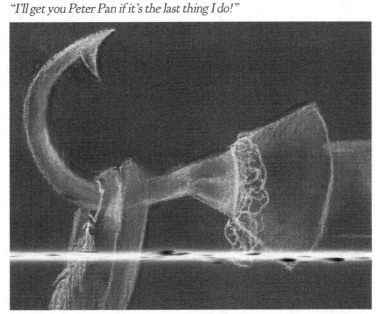

TipToe Gently

Poetry by Kate Smith, Senior
Digital Art by Mariah Rippy, Junior

He only needed, did his do,
Needed nothing never true.
Boiling fire, sickened screams,
He flourishes in their died dead dreams.

This spot he's not, with wish accrue
While the raven picks through hummingbird brew.
Grinning, grinning, Inferno enveloped,
Waiting for what's not yet developed.

Waiting, baiting, for day you do,
To pay you, weigh you, slake your you.
So tiptoe gently,
tiptoe
gently.
Tiptoe
gently.
Tip. Toe

Gently.

Gently toe tip if the edge is in view;
Never forget the misconstrued.
Just forget not, that he, the who,
The devil will sit, awaiting you.

Deepest Pit

Poetry by Jacob Hoyt, Junior

Some think I'm from earth,
a product of a human birth.
My mind is rotted from insanity;
I will eventually cause a calamity,
'cuz my father is Satan,
and I'm in hell waiting
to be released on the human slime.
I do not look capable of crime,
but I'm the definition of sin.
Your God will not win.
He will fall at my feet,
so dad won't leave his seat.
My personality is not well,
because I'm from the deepest pit of hell.

Click. Bang.

Poetry by Ayla Felix, Senior
Scholastic Writing Award Honorable Mention
Photo by Kate Smith, Senior

She stands, ever patient,
waiting for the headlights of a red Ford pickup to flash in the driveway,
waiting for the front door to swing open and let so many things in.
Her dress sticks to her like a second skin, one of black satin, from the rain.
The floor makes a small noise of protest
as she shifts her weight from one stiletto heeled foot to the other.
Her fingers play over the cold, shiny barrel of the pistol behind
her back, and she waits.
Lights flash.
The door opens.
"Hey, honey."
Click.
Bang.
"Goodbye, *darling*."

She's *done* waiting.

Sounds of a Dying Heart

Nonfiction by Abby Thacker, Junior
Oil by Kate Smith, Senior

I was awakened at 7:16 a.m. on September 11th, 2010, by my mother hovering over me. I realized instantly that something was not right by the look on her face. She asked me if I'd talked to my boyfriend Frank James Harris that morning. Reaching for my phone, the beating of my heart quickened with every beat. No messages. My mom touched my shoulder and said that Frank and his friend Marc were in a bad accident. Everything froze, and tears rolled from my worried eyes. Was he OK? Where was he now? When did this happen? Millions of questions ran through my confused mind.

Pulling myself together, I picked up the phone to call Frank's sister Amanda. She told me that the firemen at the crash sight were still trying to get the bodies out of the car. Every inch of my insides felt like they burst into a thousand pieces. More tears streamed down my already soaking face as I thought about my poor baby's body stuck in a smashed car. Minutes feel like days, and hours feel like years as I sat and waited for

the one answer I sought. Was he alive?

At 9:48 the phone rang, and my heart jumped at the sound. Mom answered the phone as I walked into the kitchen where Frank and my family have had dinner multiple times before. Walking back to the dining room where my mom and grandma were standing by the window, I saw that mom was crying, not just any kind of crying but painful crying. Deep down within me, I knew it couldn't be good, but I asked who had called. Mom turned to me with puffy eyes and said, "That was your dad. Frank's uncle called him. Abby, Frank didn't make it." I collapsed to the ground and shook in every inch of my body. The word, "No" came out of me like a broken record. My

mind went blank. The breaths I took slowed down to hardly anything. Mom told me to breathe, just keep breathing, but my body refused. I wanted to be with him. I wanted my body to be still and lifeless just like Frank's. The world meant nothing to me; my life meant nothing without him. I was lost, hurt, and confused.

I tried to sleep most of the day, but every time I woke up, I looked at my mom, praying that it was only a nightmare. Although, when our eyes met, they told me the truth, the truth that the love of my life was gone forever. More tears as I drifted back to sleep. For the rest of the weekend I cried and sat alone, thinking about every minute he and I spent together. Then it hit me; Amanda was Marc's

girlfriend. She lived in the apartment with Frank and Marc. She had it twice as bad. The loss of one loved one was already hard enough; I couldn't imagine having two loved ones pass away.

When it came to Monday, the drive to school, and not having a text saying, "I love you baby. Come see me after school," was crushing. I attempted to be strong, but there was no use. I passed a kid who had a Tapout shirt on. Memories spread though my mind like wild flowers of that Thursday, two days before the accident, when he and I laid on the couch watching UFC. It was one of Frank's favorites. He always wore a Tapout shirt when I saw him. Walking to my first hour class and seeing people in the halls laughing and having a good time just made things worse. I broke down in heavy tears standing by myself, until my ex saw me and tried to comfort me. As his arm wrapped around me, I felt a bit more safe, but his touch was unbearable compared to Frank's. Friends of mine walked by and stared, not saying a word, not stopping to save me. But sure enough, Traversa, a true friend, ran up to me and I latched onto her. Her arms held my limp body from falling to the floor.

Traveling through the halls, people stared at me like I was a crazy person. Their stares burned right through me. Later that day my other friends asked me what was wrong. I told them my news, and they both stared at me, not knowing what to say. Losing a loved one is not like a game where you can just restart; it's life and it can be final. We each must work things out on our own.

The funeral came, and I attended Marc's, but seeing all the pictures and his buddies was hard. I only stayed for the viewing, knowing that tomorrow I'd be at my love's funeral. The rest of the day my family was quiet, not saying a word. Then came Frank's funeral. We entered the church, and bulletin boards were set up with pictures of his happy life. Finally, it was time to walk up the aisle to his urn. The line went slowly, too fast for comfort, and when I looked up from the

floor, there was no one in front of me. My eyes found his senior picture on top of the box that held his ashes. Slowly stepping forward, my heart tightened with pain. Out of nowhere, a sound came out of me, the sound of sadness, hurt, and sorrow, all coming down in waterfall tears.

After that, a slide show of music and pictures streamed across a screen. A picture of him and me slid across; the day the picture was taken replayed over in my head. Pictures of him hunting rolled onto the screen. My dad, sitting next to me, let his tears fall onto my hand, for Frank was like a son to him. He knew him when he was little, and even then Frank had his bow and arrow ready to slay the big one.

After the slide show we all headed to the cemetery. There, Amanda called me to the family circle where several blue velvet chairs were arranged neatly around Frank's urn of ashes. I looked at her in disbelief and shook my head, letting her know I couldn't do it but she insisted. She said that Frank would like to look

down upon us all and see me as part of his family. Walking to a blue velvet chair, she and I sat hand and hand with a wadded up tissue in the other.

Days go by like nothing happened, but scars are left on everyone. Many people never realize how important something is until they lose it, especially if that "something" is someone you love very deeply. It's hard to believe if you haven't experienced anything like this before, but the experience is like having your flesh torn from your body. The pain just eats away until there is nothing left. So here I am living my life day by day, waiting without fear to die

and be with my baby once again. To see his smile and feel his touch once more is way beyond a wish or an answered prayer; it's heaven. I will never forget him and how he changed my life.

For now, I will continue to stay strong about the tragedy that happened and will always remember the amazing times he and I had together. Cherish the ones you love every waking minute you have because you never know when they will leave you. This is my life, and this is my story, letting everyone know that life is short, so live it to the very fullest.

~In Loving Memory of Frank James Harris~

A Cruel Trick of a Treat

Nonfiction Satire by Aaron Stegemiller, Senior
Pencil by Anna Schmalzried, Junior

There are many American customs that would cause an alien to tilt and scratch his or her bulbous head. One of the most outrageous customs is the "holiday" of Halloween. Who would come up with a day to celebrate the things we most fear? How could such a Satanic ritual be so acceptable in our culture? Oh, wait a second. I know the answer to that last question. Free candy! Nobody can turn that down. It is human nature to accept and then horde any form of sweet tasting food. Candy begs to be eaten and we're happy to oblige. So what if we recognize and celebrate the devil along the way?

Throughout our childhood, we are taught two things. Number one: Don't talk to strangers and number two: Don't take candy from strangers. These simple rules are pounded into our minds by our protective mothers. But apparently on Halloween, all bets are off and the potential of finding a sweet and salty Snickers bar is worth the risk of finding Herbert the Pervert. I imagine there are a lot of older, single men who enjoy the children's costumes a little too much, but hey, they have good candy right? Let's think of the easiest scenario for child abduction. My guess is that it would be nighttime, the child would be by him or herself, both the abductor and the abductee would be disguised so that tracing would be more difficult, the child would approach the adult, not vice-versa, and the setting would be noisy. What do you know, I just unknowingly described evenings on October 31st of every year. The complete recklessness of Halloween is flabbergasting.

Overall, Halloween is a sorry excuse for a holiday. In fact, it is just an excuse for us to get free food and not feel badly about it. They say all "good" things must come to an end, but those whiny, piggy little children will make sure that Halloween is not one of them.

[[Creative Sparks]]

Careful Balance
of Egotistic Minds

Poetry by Lauren Kipper, Senior
Watercolor by Seth Baker, Senior

As they meander down the halls,
their heads made of combustive matter,
they keep to themselves
because too much contact with another would ruin
their perfect balance.
Heads would start exploding.
One after another.
Their atmospheres would drop to the ground
and
mush together.
The people on the tiny planets in their atmospheres
would be forced to be extroverted,
learn about another
and
maybe even care.
No!
This could happen.
"We cannot let ourselves be vulnerable!" their little mayors scream.
So they keep this distance as they meander down the hallways
going on with their lives, never wondering what would happen
if just maybe once they thought about an atmosphere beyond their

o

w

n.

Forever No Longer

Poetry by Breanna Kretchmer, Senior
Photo by Kate Smith, Senior

I can still feel it,
your ice cold hands like clamps on my shoulders,
hollow black eyes burning into mine,
your stone heart thumping wildly.
Your voice like a knife
drove into me,
the words filled my mind,
turning it all to mush.
I was falling,
hard.
Your insincere smile
promised me forever,
yet forever was gone,
and no one could stop it.
I was drowning in your pool of lies,
no way out.
The voice in the back of my head
screamed *Don't do it.*
Like a flashing neon sign,
it told me it was wrong;
I didn't listen.
Like a tiger you sank you claws in,
deeply,
under my skin.
I felt the fire in your touch,
I melted like putty in your clutch.
I woke in the morning to the unforgiving sun,
I felt the pain.
What's done is done,
and I can still feel it.

Always Here

Poetry Renga by Mariah Rippy,
Junior; Chantell Cooper, Junior;
Nick Havranek, Junior;
and Kirsten Brown, Junior
Oil by Allison Adkins, Senior

You think I'm gone,
out of your hair.
Think again, boy,
I'm always here.

See me now,
as you saw me at first.
I'm here and never leaving,
only way to sate a thirst.

Dripping wet with fear,
I'll never change you.
You only have eyes for me,
I'll never chain you.

Just listen to my voice
Or unleash my wrath.
This could be simple;
you choose your path.

EXPLOSIVE CHEMISTRY

"Love is a fire. But whether it is going to warm your hearth or burn down your house, you can never tell." - Joan Crawford

Feel the heat of passion and desire, the warmth of love of family...

What It Is

*Poetry Renga by Autumn Ladyga, Senior;
Mariah Rippy, Junior; Jacob Hoyt, Junior;
and Ariel Clark, Junior
Pencil by Lina Hennig, Junior*

Love is a spark
that attaches to
your heart and
sends a smile to
your face; embrace.

Passion is a fruit
that hangs by
its roots and
releases butterflies to
your core; adore.

Romance is a rare thing
that brings joy
with every word said
causing cartwheels inside when
your stomach turns; passion burns.

Desire is a tingle
that brings alive
every cell within and
makes you feel like
a peaceful dove; love.

Vibrations

Poetry Renga by Jenna Luczyk, Junior;
Olivia Hurley, Senior; Emily Thomas, Senior;
and Chantell Cooper, Junior
Watercolor by Blake Harris, Senior

When you walk into the room,
you light up everything.
There is a spell that comes over me,

a spell I cannot seem to break.
It flows like electricity through me,
overcoming me, unbreakable, as I

stumble over my words
when your gaze trips me impolitely,
yet your smile lifts me off the ground again.
Your kind lips kiss my forehead
and my eyes become a flame,

a flame that lights every cell.

a sound so melodic that I fall under your spell.
My heart vibrates to that sweet chord.

The Life of Mr. Chevrolet

Nonfiction by Kelsey Mitschelen, Senior
Photo of Kelsey Mitschelen's Grandfather in his Chevy at
the Chicago Amphitheater indoor track, January, 5, 1964

I can't imagine how I would have turned out if I didn't have him around in my life. In almost all of my childhood memories, he is there. Teaching or showing me something, protecting me from danger, singing to me, making me the most delicious foods ever. He taught me to drive, he opened my taste to different foods, he's taken me camping several times, and has done so much more for me. His influence helped me become who I am today. He has always been there for me. I never have to worry about doing something wrong or unacceptable in the eyes of everyone else because I know that he will love me no matter what. The person I am talking about goes by many names. His name is Brother to his eleven siblings, Father to his nine kids, Pa to his twenty grandchildren, and Great-Grandpa to his two great-grandchildren. His name is Mr. Chevrolet to his racing buddies. To his friends and family his name is Red. To the world his name is Herman Williams, and he is my grandpa. I have never really known about my grandfather's past. He is very modest and never really felt the need to tell anyone about it. But that has changed in the past few years.

When my grandpa was a young teenager, speed was accepted.

It was actually encouraged by the car makers; they made commercials advertising cars that could exceed speeds of 150 miles per hour. Of course, my grandpa had to have one. A 1963 Chevy Biscayne became his best friend. He wanted and needed speed which led him to win over a thousand races. He started racing on US 31 right outside Lakeville. The number of people who would come see the races easily reached a hundred; of course, they couldn't stay long because of the fear that they might get caught by the police. Soon he moved up to racing at the Osceola track and the indoor racing track in Chicago that used to be called Soldier Field. It was at these drag strips that he went on to win his class 48 times in a season and a half, setting a major record. At the peak of his racing career, he was even offered a chance to participate in making a commercial with the owner of the Osceola drag strip. Anytime he spoke of racing, it was with excitement in his eyes, and he would always say," It's more than drag racing; it's a way of life."

When he started settling down, he decided it was time to sell his car. The motor was taken from the car and put into a boat that was the fastest boat on The Lake of the

Woods for over twenty years. Now, he simply owns a clone of his original car. It's a car that looks exactly the same as the first one but doesn't have the same experience.

My grandpa is an amazing man. He never really learned what it means to lose, and not just in his racing career but in life, too. After he left the race tracks, he started a large family that loves him dearly. Over the years that family grew and so did their love for him. But his careless lifestyle was soon tested. He suffered a massive heart attack. His bad eating habits, smoking, and heavy drinking landed him in the hospital. After a quick recovery, he was back at home and enjoying life once again. Of course, he had to make a few minor changes in his life. He began eating correctly and lost weight quickly. He also successfully quit smoking, which is a challenge all on its own.

A few years later he was burdened with cancer. The doctors found a tumor on his kidney. He was in the hospital recovering for weeks. I was worried that I wouldn't have my grandpa anymore. He was forced to have surgery to they remove the tumor before the cancer could spread. He didn't seem like the same person sitting there in his hospital gown, but that changed after a month or so. He was able to leave the hospital where he finished his recovery at home. He regained his strength, and started doing the things he loved again. It may seem like he's had it rough, but in these situations, he did win; he beat each one.

This past October, he turned 71. But unlike any other 71 year old who might just have a small family gathering, my grandpa decided to celebrate his own way. He took his 1963 Biscayne clone and went to the Osceola track. This track is only about a quarter of a mile long, but that didn't stop him from reaching high speeds. In 14.8 seconds he was able to make it to the finish line and reached a speed of 100.25 miles per hour. That day he smiled as he remembered his old racing days. He's always had the heart of a child. That's what makes him Grandpa.

Every year grandpa takes us grandkids, and we drive down to his mother's old property and go mushroom hunting. Whenever he finds one, he steps right over it so that one of us kids can have the chance to find our very own morel mushroom. We would know whenever he just found one because he would over exaggerate that one step, and we would all go running for it.

When I was little, he would put me on the four wheeler, and he would sit right behind me. We would find some of the muddiest pits to play in and the steepest hills to

climb. We had so much fun, but he always made sure that no harm came to me. He even taught me to drive. I began learning around the age of four. I would sit on his lap as he pressed the gas while I steered. My cousins and I call the car in which he taught us to drive the Isuzu. The Isuzu never had brakes. When I got older and to the point where I didn't need to sit on his lap, he would tell me to slow down drastically so that I could stop. I would get confused

when I pressed the brake pedal that didn't work. I will never forget the moment when he told me to " just run it into that tree over there." Yup, that's my grandpa and that's what I did. Of course, I was never going fast enough to hurt anyone when I did run it into the tree.

To this day whenever I call him on the phone to talk to him, he can't end our conversation. If I attempt to say goodbye to him, he refuses to hang up. He will quickly hand the phone to Grandma so she can say goodbye. The thought of

hanging up on me kills him; he just can't do it.

Ever since I can remember, my grandpa has always loved speed. You can usually find him on a motorcycle, three wheeler, four wheeler, jeep, or just about anything with wheels. I never knew of his teenage years when he would race on drag strips and win trophies. Even at the age 71, he still acts childish sometimes. When I go to his house, he makes me a specials pot of

his famous chicken and noodles, and as he stands over the boiling pot, he sings random songs in a mocking opera voice. I know that I can always run to him if I need help. He's my grandpa, and the memory of him is embedded in my mind. I just hope that the day will never come when all I have of my grandpa is a faint memory of him. I never want to hang up for good.

Where I'm Coming From

Poetry by Kirsten Brown, Junior
Scholastic Writing Gold Key Award
Charcoal by Emily Thomas, Senior

I am from the protection of a woman
Firmly grasping my hand,
From the watchful eyes of a man
Fearlessly guarding my soul

I am from the August sun,
Cool sprinklers on a blazing summer day,
From fields of mown blue grass
Parachuting seeds from dandelions

I am from freedom of speech
And speaking my mind,
From a stroll in their shoes
And gladly giving my time

I am from patience and waiting
For life's next proposal,
From practice makes perfect
And navigating the stars

I am from confusion
And blind rage,
From pure tranquility
And the frequent tinkle of laughter

I am from the warmest past
And a warmer future,
From hopes and desires
And granted wishes

I am from many others,
But I am only myself,
From rapidly changing times
And constant love

Beautiful BRAVE One

Nonfiction by Jake Ayala, Senior
Charcoal by Kaylee Bruggeman, Sophomore

There she was, Rachel Connelly, as beautiful as the summer night sky, as it played with the neon colorfulness of the stars and the moon. It was my first day in St. Michaels, and

I was just transferred in from another country, Saudi Arabia. Now there are two pieces of information I can give you if you are a "mover kid" like I was. The first is golden: never talk the first day unless someone talks to you; and second: above all, remember that little kids are ruthless.

So there I was the first day, in my Catholic school uniform, new book bag, and brand new white shoes that squeaked a little bit when I walked. I sat there awkwardly at my desk, playing with a little dinosaur pencil eraser. I was so alone. I missed my mom and my dad, but above all I missed the country I had grown used to.

As the bell rang, I felt my guts turn to ice, and my mouth grew very dry. As the kids came in, they all smiled at me. Looking back, I know the teacher made them all do it. "Who's the new kid?" Chad Bowlog, ladies and gentlemen. I promised myself that one day I'd write a fairy tale and he would be a troll, an evil, vicious troll; anything to tarnish the memory of a school bully.

"I'm Jake Ayala. I'm from Saudi Arabia!" First mistake.

"Wait! The guys who blew up our towers?" I looked down.

"Yes, my dad taught the Arabian Air Force how to fly." They all sat looking at me, open mouthed.

"Meet us at recess. We want a show you something."

I was ecstatic, my first real friends. Class went on, and Rachel Connelly walked in, like I said, as beautiful as ever. She caught my eye for one second, and only one. I stared though. How could I not? She was, as my dad called them, a "hey babies."

Finally, recess came, and I literally ran out to the playground. There they sat, the cool guys.

"Hey fellas I-" I was cut off

very quickly.

"Look, terrorist, I want you gone! You ain't gonna kill anyone here." I was shocked.

"I'm not a bomber, fellas. I'm just a kid like you."

Chad paused, then said, "You ain't nothing like me. You ain't a kid; you're a terrorist! And what do we do with terrorists, boys?" I felt a tear run down my cheek. "We kill em!" They all pounced on me, and hit me all over. Now I don't really remember well, but someone must have been stabbing a puppy because that sound flooded my ears. Finally, I could see the sky again. I got up, dusted myself off, and wiped away the tears and blood.

"Look, Jake, I know where you're from. Put them past you. They're guys, after all. Stupid ones, true. You be Jake; be the better person. I'll talk to them. Don't worry. Keep your head up, okay?" The most beautiful sound I've ever heard, Rachael Connelly.

Over the years it got a little better, but for four years, I received the worst abuse I'd ever received. I kept her words in my head though. It kept me going though all those years. It kept me going through all the names, racial slurs, and hatred. That girl was my first love for showing me in just a few simple words, how to endure and how life really should be and can be.

"Hate and force cannot be in just a part of the world without having an effect on the rest of it." -Eleanor Roosevelt

The Way I Smiled

Nonfiction by Emily Thomas, Senior
Scholastic Writing Gold Key
Charcoal by Ayla Felix, Senior

When I was a child, I danced quite often, especially when the summer nights were brimming with stars and the fireflies would hover just out of my reach. I would try catching them, but if I ever succeeded, I would let them go again. I remember the feel of tiny legs and wings inside my clenched hands, and I would laugh because it tickled me. Once, when I was about six or so, I was running about with my older brother, Clayton. He was eight years older than me, much too old to play anymore, but on this particular night we were having fun in the yard. My grandma and mom were sitting on the porch, watching my brother and I kick around a Barbie ball. I was a roughish child, dressed in a red jumper and bare feet, my blonde hair knotted. The fireflies were thick, flying in swarms, lighting up in patterns, as though they were fireworks bursting in the night sky. I recall Clayton catching one and smashing the insect on my ball; Barbie's face glowed in a green smear. It was sticky and neon, and I was oddly repulsed and fascinated by what my brother had done.

A few summers went by, and I was starting my first year in 4H. I lived on a farm with cattle and sheep, so it was only natural that I was involved in the program. I had been showing livestock since I was a toddler. I remember my father and I walking in a field, looking at baby calves. One sleek red calf caught my eye and walked in my direction. He licked my hand, the slobber feeling sticky, just as the firefly smear had, so I patted his nose and rubbed his back. His tongue felt very soft and wet on my fingers. I felt so at ease with the calf, and I couldn't contain my smile. My dad chuckled and

said that I should have brought maple syrup with me, for a calf would always lick your hand if you had maple syrup. My eyes grew big at this information, and I laughed, thinking about my baby calf eating a breakfast of pancakes and OJ instead of cut grass and corn silage.

As I woke many years later, I smelled the same maple syrup from my past, calling me to breakfast. My mother made waffles with strawberries and whipped cream, syrup and apple juice. It was a Saturday morning and the sunlight was filtered through the windows in my kitchen, giving off a warm glow. My mother looked so happy in her pajamas, melting the butter on the waffle iron. The TV was playing on the counter, the news or something. I believe that it was snowing. My brother was home from college, and my entire family went to the farm to do the morning chores. Because of the deep snow drifts, my dad plowed the barnyard, making a huge glistening heap of snow to the left of the barn. The heap of snow was about eight feet tall and quite wide, making it perfect for a steep and short ride on a sledding saucer. My brother and I slid down the small mountain, and as we hit the ice on the driveway, we would spin uncontrollably, the wind biting our cheeks and causing dizzy euphoria.

Later on, the wind bit my face again as I pulled my wool hat down over my ears. I was around fourteen, and I had gone with the school to Swiss Valley ski resort. I had never been skiing before that day, but I learned quickly and I was at the top of a mountain with my friend Michelle. We looked down at the perilous edge of the Black Diamond, the most advanced mountain. To say I was an

intermediate level skier was a giant overstatement, but here I was, perched like a bird on a tree branch, ready to fly or fall to the bottom. Michelle and I pushed off and we tumbled almost immediately. The slope was so steep that it seemed almost vertical, and we fell down two-thirds of the mountain. When we finally skidded to a stop in a tumbled heap, I had lost my hat, one boot, both of my skis and I had snow in every crevice and orifice. Strangely, we were fine and unscathed. Michelle and I started to laugh, in a disoriented manner, as our breath made clouds of condensation around our snowy heads.

Just as my breath made swirls in the winter air, the sugar in my lemonade made swirls when I whisked my straw in the yellow cup. It was the summer I turned seventeen and my friends were about to sneak into a concert at the county fair. I tossed my empty cup before I tried to follow them through the crowds, but alas, they lost me. For a moment, I was alone, until I saw a boy wearing bright green, Converse high top sneakers. His name was Brenden, I knew this much, and he was a friend of a friend. I had met him earlier that week.

"Hey, Brenden!" I said to him. He replied back, and we chatted a bit before I saw someone else walk by Brenden's side. He was taller than me, with heavily lidded eyes, the color of a pond or mountain-clear, green and blue. He had a wide smile fitted with braces and a TSC hat upon his brown blond hair. He held his hand out to me, introducing himself. I was immediately aware of how polite this kid was.

"Hi!" he said, looking at Brenden questioningly. "And who is this?" he asked me, sticking out his hand. It occurred to me that no one under the age of forty ever shook my hand upon meeting me.

This kid is something else, I thought to myself. I shook his rough hand, and replied, "I'm Emily. And I lost my friends, because they're dumb and they snuck into the concert and I can't get a hold of them."

"Well", the boy smiled, "you just made two new ones. I am Sam. Want to walk around? I'm hungry. Let's get something to eat."

The three of us walked around the fair, chatting and getting to know each other. I began to realize that Sam Brown was unlike any other guy I had ever met. He was clean cut, and liked to do things for others like pay for deep fried cookie dough (the food we shared together on the first night.) He would pick up trash off the ground or open doors for little old ladies. Sam was a gentleman, and something about him made me never want to leave him, not even to go home in the evening. He was chivalrous, and we were falling for each other pretty hard. I asked my friend for his number the first night, and we texted each other long into the morning.

Since I met him on a Thursday at fair, we only had two days left to be together. He came every day, just to see me. For some inexplicable reason, he felt the same way I did about him. We would sit beneath a tree on the outskirts of the fair and watch as people walked my. I remember the shadows on his face as the tree branches blew and fluttered the leaves in the breeze. We would talk about everything: our favorite drinks, what life meant, our favorite movies, what we wanted to do when we grew up, and what we feared. He told me he was frightened of storms, and this

"I was around seven or so," he told me, "and it was storming like crazy. There were tornado warnings,

and my family had a dog at the time." I remembered this storm when he retold it. I was in about second grade at the time; he was in first. "Well, the dog was outside and my family was in the cellar, and they sent me out to get the stupid thing. I had to search in the rain, with twisters in plain sight on the horizon. I was scared shitless. I finally got the dog and ran down the stairs with him. I was crying pretty hard, too." He trailed off.

In my mind, I recalled all of the fun times I had when summer storms came. One happened that very same summer. I was with my friend Erika, and we were in her empty house when the power went out and the thunder started rolling. We both adored storms, but it was dark in the house and we couldn't find flashlights. Meticulously, we gathered all of the candles in the house. There were birthday candles, giant Yankee candles, and tiny white circular candles with black wicks. We lit every candle, over forty in all, and arranged them in a circle. We called it the witch's circle, and the room became blazing hot smelled of wax and scents with the candles. The thunder boomed once again, and we all shrieked in surprise.

It felt as though the house was shaking in the storm. We screamed again and started laughing uncontrollably. Storms, no matter how loud, don't frighten me. I retold the story to Sam, and when I finished, the festering sky let out a low rumble of thunder.

We ran to a nearby barn and stood under its eaves. At that moment, rain began to pour down in bucket fulls, and the barn's tin roof made pattering sounds as the water hit the metal. It was beautiful, and the sky was a strange shade of pink as the summer rain made puddles in the street. I pulled him outside, against his will. I smiled and started to dance in the water. We were both laughing now.

I danced; he smiled. It was as though I was young again, dancing with the fireflies. My head turned up to the sky and a grin spread upon my face. I knew right then that he was going to play a major part in my life. We wrote each other letters after that night. I called him often, and we visited each other a few times. However the distance between his house and mine was great, and time made us forget our feelings for one another. We had to work at our love, but in the end, we couldn't deny the fireflies in our hearts. Whenever I see him now, I still get the same feeling as I did the first time. My heart spins as though I am still dancing in the rain, as though I am still tumbling down a mountain, as though I am still playing with my brother, or as though I am still in the field with my calf.

He makes me feel alive and young again. As we danced in the rain, hand in hand, I saw in the corner of my eye an elderly couple slow dancing under the roof of the nearby candy shop. Our eyes met for an instant, and the couple smiled. I began to wonder if had, and if when we grew old, I would still dance like a child in the rain.

Subject of a Masterpiece

Poetry by Danielle Wroblewski, Senior
Charcoal by Brandi Burkhart, Sophomore
Scholastic Art Award Silver Key

He shades her eyes with iridescent hues,
Paints a rose upon her lips and cheek.
The sky looms above his love, a brilliant blue,
As he creates her portrait, so fragile and weak.
Her luminous blonde curls cascade down her neck,
Skin as soft as baby's breath and sigh.
A single night without her and he's a wreck,
His entire being transfixed by the look in her eyes.
A complexion so ethereal, a pale and pure white,
Her touch so soothing, remedies a broken man's curse.
For her love, any man he'll fight,
He'll love her forever, for better or for worse.
      She's the only woman who can capture his heart,
      And the only subject to his never-ending art.

Breaking Composure

Poetry by Kelsey Piotrowicz, Senior
Oil by Ayla Felix, Senior

Current run to my fingertips
and cause the storm to begin in my stomach.
The fairytale setting is dark for only this small time.
The curtain, like a comforter, keeps me safe in this momentary solitude.
The smell of paint, wood, and old fabric waltzes at my nose.
      I must remember to be someone else.
It's a different time, different place, a different mindset.
The low mumble of people in their seats can still be heard over the boisterous band.
Familiar melodies dance and glide from one to another in harmony.
However, the familiarity only causes the winds to pick up their pace inside me.
"Break a leg!" someone whispers.
I'm sure I'll break something.
What was that line? Crap.
Just remember, I am me *and* her.
The thunder begins as my pulse quickens its step and rings in my ears.
A few deep breaths are needed to prevent fainting.
The music comes to the right place.
Blindingly, luminous lights begin to shine
with blazing warmth.
      Oh, shit.
      This is it.

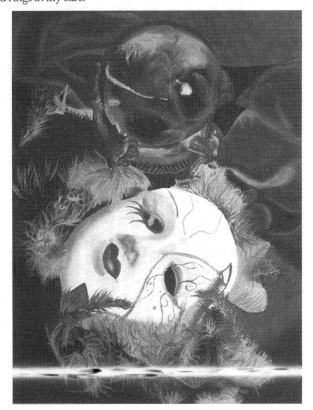

Nonfiction by Autumn Rose Ladyga, Senior
Oil by Kate Smith, Senior

The Loss of a

I was young: 9 years old. For being that young, I had already been through a lot more than some kids ever have to go through, but those stories aren't what this is about. This is about May 23rd, the day that I lost my father.

May 22nd was a typical day as far as I was concerned. The sky was still above the ground and the sun was still shining. Nothing seemed unusual. It was a Wednesday, and that meant that after school, Dad would have visitation with us kids from 5 until 9. My dad was never really good with sticking to visitation.

My dad was a tall, dark-haired, dark-skinned man. The only reason that he was dark-skinned was because he worked construction and was out on the intense heat for most days. He was handy like that. Most of all though, he was flaky about being on time to get us kids most of the time, and left us in pure disappointment.

However, on this one specific Wednesday, Dad was right on time, with enthusiasm all over his face. I couldn't remember the last time that I had seen my dad like that. He looked eager and excited to spend time with my brother, sisters, and me. Seeing him all pumped up just got us in a great mood!

Usually, Dad took us all the way to Walkerton from our apartment in Mishawaka on Wednesdays, which gave us more time in the car than actually spending time together at his house. But for some reason, he decided that he just wanted to buy us McDonald's and take us to the park on that day. To us, the idea was amazing, because it gave us more time to have fun, and less time to be cramped together in his little Hornet car.

Playing at the park was the most fun that we had had in a long time. I know that might sound sad, but it was true. Whenever we were with Dad, it seemed like there was so much awkward tension, but at the same time, we loved him. He was our dad. The afternoon quickly turned to evening, and it was time to go. We actually got home late because we were having so much fun, and to our surprise, Mom didn't mind. She was just happy that Dad was putting so much effort into spending time with us now, as opposed to ditching us like he usually did.

When we got out of the car, instead of running up to Mom like we did on those countless Wednesday nights, we walked over to Dad and all gave him good night kisses. He always gave the sloppiest kisses because of the overload of Carmex on his lips. We all said, "I love you," and then Melissa, my older sister, told him to drive safely. Little did we know, that was the very last time that we were going to see our dad alive.

The following day was fine, as far as I was concerned. I actually was busy planning a sleepover that I was about to have that upcoming Friday. So, the day was agreeable, and then the night fell over me like a blanket. I fell asleep in my room with my sisters, and then my brother came and slept in there with us, too. He did that sometimes. By 10 o'clock that night, Mom was in our room waking us all up. We were groggy and hardly awake. Quite honestly, she just told us what happened, in the most calming and considerate way that she could.

Instantly, tears swarmed our eyes and we all thought that it was just a dream. We migrated downstairs and sat awake on the couch, crying, while Mom called all of our relatives and Dad's relatives from the home phone in the hallway. All that I really remember about that night and about what I was feeling was that I was lost. My dad was gone, and I'd never see him again. I'd never get mad at him again, and I'd never sit on his lap again.

That tragedy changed my life at such a young age. It showed me that loved ones come and go. You can sulk in the loss forever, or you can learn to overcome it and learn from the loss. My dad, dying from a drunken car accident, has been my main motivation to keep my head on straight. His death has been my inspiration to defeat the peer pressure and to make my own level-headed decisions. My dad will never be able to get defensive about a boyfriend or to even walk me down the aisle at my wedding, but his life and his love has helped me to grow as a person, and I'll always remember him.

Loved One

FAMILY TIME

Nonfiction by Mark Davis, Senior
Charcoal by Meredith Rogers, Junior

It's a process that takes some time; sign here, run there, "have you ever...?" Joining the military seems like a simple thing to do, but I assure you that it is not. You have to run all over the MEPS (Military Entrance Processing Station) building to fill out paperwork, fingerprint yourself, sign your name, and even get a complete physical. It's a hectic procedure, and it's very boring. I guess that moment when you finish all your paperwork and you're beginning to swear in, you realize that maybe it happened a little too fast. That endurance test of your mental stability that seemed to take forever just ended with a complete stop, without warning.

What will I do? I am leaving a week after graduation, and I have so many things I want to do. But is there enough time? I want to have fun and see my family, but if I leave, I may never have the chance to tell them I love them again or that everything will be all right. It just digs a hole in my chest that burns more and more every time I think about it. My girlfriend and I have only been together for two months at this point, but for some reason, it seems like I'm just abandoning her so soon. I want her to wait for me, and I know she will, but there is so much that we should do before I leave. But not enough time, not enough time. So here I am, trying to make every minute worthwhile, and have fun and enjoy every second of my life.

As the days count down, I realize that I'm leaving in a few months, and I've been spending all my time with those who are close to me. Most of it has been with my girlfriend, and it seems as if we are married already. We basically spend enough time together that if you were to add it up, it would probably be like we do live together. That's not a problem to me though. I enjoy her company, and I enjoy the times we have. I'm going to miss the memories while I'm gone, and it's going to keep me going when I'm over there and in a tight spot. There isn't a moment in the day I go with thoughts of her running through my head.

"Family is all you have," my father always says. No one else will care for you or see you the way they will. I love that about my dad. He can be an ass at times, but he'll tell me straight up that he loves me and that he doesn't want me to become some foot/grunt soldier "taking bullets for some old prick in the states who can't fight his own fight." He loves me so much that he just gets upset and angry when I talk about leaving. I'm valuing the time we spend together now. Whether he realizes it or not, it's going to be hard for him. My mother, as well, doesn't want to see me come back in casket, and I don't blame her. The thought of having to bury her child terrifies her. And then there's my little sister. I never realized how much she looked up to me until she came home from school, upset that she didn't get the number jersey she wanted for basketball. She wanted number 11, and she said she wanted it because her big brother wore 11 for football. Coming from her, that meant a lot. My brother, I envy for his brain and intelligence. He could read a book and tell you word for word about any page. It's hard knowing what he thinks most the time, but I feel as if he doesn't want me to go.

It's tough looking at them and knowing that I'm leaving so soon. I have too much to do and so little time. So I'm here just making it worth it. From every goodnight to every good morning.

Without You

Poetry by Ariel Clark, Junior
Watercolor by Meredith Rogers, Junior

The wind howls,
the trees sigh,
the river whispers its sweet lullaby.
As the wind dies down,
the trees at rest,
my mind begins to wonder.
Reminiscing my sweet memories,
wishing you were somehow here with me,
asking myself why you're gone,
still wishing you'd come back home.
As time passes, your memory fades,
the memories that were once so clear seem hazed.
Though your memories fade,
my love for you will remain the same.
Remembering can bring me sorrow,
always wishing you would show up tomorrow
smiling like you always do,
showing me everything will be okay,
wishing I had you one last day.
Stupid me,
wishing things that can never be.
Before I know it,
I look up and realize the sun has set,
and all that's left to do is survive
another long day without you.

EAST RACE

Nonfiction by Megan Beery, Senior

Charcoal by Amanda Bachtel, Senior

Scholastic Art Award Silver Key

HE'D been my best friend for the past year and a half. At the time, that's all I thought we'd ever be. We'd talk every night for a couple of hours, and every Saturday we'd go to South Bend for some fun. For me, these Saturdays were paradise. We loved to go for long walks and look at the fall colors that were painted across the trees. This specific walk was taken in downtown South Bend at the East Race. We'd left my apple red pickup in the parking lot and headed down to the river. The sun was bright, so much so that I'd put on a pair of sunglasses to shield my eyes from its intensity. The air was pleasantly warm, yet crisp with the season's anticipated change, and it wafted gently around us, playing with our clothes and my hair. We walked close, our shoulders bumping as we headed towards my favorite spot on this part of the river. Our hands grazed past each other, an unintentional physical touch filled with electricity and the promise of what could be, if we let it. Our paces matched, despite the fact that he is seven inches taller than me. I could feel the tension between us, one that spoke the longing between us more loudly than we ever could. His steady breathing and patient silence reminded me of another time, one in which I hardly even knew him.

My grandmother, with whom I'd been living, had died suddenly the day before I was supposed to start attending a new school. I begged to be allowed to stay home, to be able to mourn her death in the solitude that I so dearly craved. My father insisted that I begin on time, regardless of our loss. He thought that going to school would help me keep my mind off of everything. I remember my first day at that small Michigan school, how it had all passed so quickly. I went through my classes in a blur, not bothering to remember the names of my teachers or the brave students who'd introduced themselves to me. I glared at anyone who attempted to approach me. They all tried to speak to me. I hadn't meant to be antisocial, but I was so lost knowing that my favorite grandmother wouldn't be waiting for me to get home. She wouldn't be anticipating my return, eager to look over me with her inquisitive, blue eyes. I knew that there would be no snack of wheat thins and port cheese with her after school, as had been our habit, and that I would have to plan dinner without her from now on.

Her death meant so much more than one less place setting at the dinner table. It meant that while my mother spent long hours away from the house looking for a new home for

our family with my father, I would have to be the woman of the house. I would help my little sister Olivia with homework; I would care for the dogs. Alone, I would now care for my grandfather who had Alzheimer's, and my mentally handicapped, epileptic uncle Paul. They would need me to make certain that they took their meds and ate all their food. To say that I felt overwhelmed is probably one of the most exaggerated understatements ever applied to my life. School was always second to my family; it had become a frustration that stole seven hours a day away from me. Seven hours that could be better spent making sure that everything would be in order when my parents got home. It's not that they ever asked me to do this; it was a task that I stepped up to willingly, knowing that someone had to care for the family while they were trying to secure our future.

As the weeks progressed into months, I began to open up at school, but only he could actively engage me in a conversation. When I think about it, only he really cared to put forth the effort. I never questioned why he was always there for me, why he was ever ready to help me try to sort through my rocky relationship with my boyfriend at the time, or why he held me while I cried. Not once did

I stop to wonder why he constantly greeted me warmly, regardless of the way that I'd treated him the previous day. We ate lunch together everyday, and with time his friends became my friends, too. After we ate, we developed the habit of wandering the halls together, even though we weren't supposed to leave the cafeteria. No one ever stopped us from leaving, and whenever a teacher stopped us in the hall to send us back to the cafeteria, we would act like we were going back, but instead we'd duck into a side hallway and continue to wander aimlessly. Slowly, steadily, this Michigan boy was healing all my scars.

I found that I looked forward to seeing his charismatic silver eyes, the ones that silently promised that he would listen to me, that he would always understand what I was saying before I'd said it. I'd affectionately explained his ability to do this because he had two sisters and was able to speak "girl" fluently. What I didn't realize at the time was that he wasn't able to speak "girl," he was able to speak "Megan." I adored his soft brown curls and the way that he would let them fall haphazardly into his face, making him look incredibly child-like. I would study with fascination his various tattoos, listening intently to the stories behind them and what they meant to him. I began to memorize everything about him, and I realized all too late that I had begun to fall in love with him. How could I not? He'd been all that I could ever need before I needed it. His chiseled, masculine face and impressive form guaranteed him a throng of admirers. At any given time three to four girls at school claimed crushes or affections for him. Yet he had chosen to spend his time putting me into one piece again. He was well-spoken, often pausing for quiet a few moments before

he answered someone's question. He seemed to think everything through to the point that most of us would find tedious. It wasn't that it took him that long to come up with a response. He just wanted to make sure that what he was saying was what you needed to hear at the moment, whether you wanted to hear it or not.

Eventually, I had to tell him that I was going to return to Indiana, after spending only one semester at Brandywine. I expected him to draw away from me, to emotionally distance himself as I knew all my other friends would. I knew that was what I would have done in that situation. Just as he'd done earlier in the year by being the only one persistent enough to bring me out of my shell, he became the exception to all that I expected. He pushed in, rather than pulling away. He began to write me lengthy notes, and he wanted to know everything about me. It was then that I began to spend more time talking with him than I did with my boyfriend Trey. He seemed to have a solution to every problem that I'd deal with. Trey said he was the genius behind many of the

conversations that temporarily healed our dysfunctional relationship. We spent time together outside of school, and gradually I let him into my personal life. I let him meet Olivia, my grandfather, and Paul; he showed me nothing but endearing qualities as he unwearyingly reintroduced himself to my grandfather time and again. I had him meet my prized possessions, my horses. I began to teach him how to relate to them, as he clumsily learned how to ride. He was everything that I'd always needed and never knew how much I'd wanted until I'd found it. It was as if he thought that he could stop me from leaving if he could make me happy there.

My family left Niles that December, and we moved into a five acre horse ranch in Walkerton, where we could keep all of our horses at home with us, rather than boarding them as we had done before. I promised him that we would still be friends when I left and that I'd never forget him. January brought unforeseeable chaos into my life as my grandfather inexplicably, required more of my parents' time. I had not adjusted well to the school that I started going to. I'd began to behave the same way that I had when I first started going to the Brandywine, shutting out my teachers and fellow students as I receded into myself. This time, though, there was no one to bring me out. Trey became more demanding, insisting that if I truly cared for him, I would spend all my free time with him and that I would give everything I had to save our relationship.

Life got in the way of my once sincere promises, and by March, I'd completely forgotten my Michigan boy. My life became pandemonium without his gentle, soothing silver eyes and comforting embrace. I couldn't understand why everything had become so different than it was while we lived in Niles. There was no logical reason for me to be more troubled now than I was after my grandmother's death. And yet I was utterly lost. I couldn't stop the flow of overwhelming feelings; I couldn't tell up from down, or even sort through the maze of my own emotions. My life became a torrent of my own self – perpetuating problems, most of them centering on Trey. I was left empty and needy, without a clue what I needed. I would spend ten months this way.

I was out running errands with my mother and Olivia one suffocating, August afternoon. As an introvert, I used to crave time alone so I could think and try to sort through things. I had given up on sorting through my life after I finally broke up with Trey. It had been months since I'd wanted to be alone. As we pulled into the grocery store parking lot, I asked if it was all right if I waited for them in the truck, driven by a strange desire to be alone for a moment. I couldn't explain why I'd suddenly had the urge to be quiet, to be able to try

and make sense of everything one more time, but it was too great for me to overcome, so I let my family go into the store without me.

I leaned back against the soft, navy upholstery of the truck, feeling the sun's warmth as it filtered in through the dark, tinted windows. Soon, I became uncomfortably hot, and began to regret my decision to stay behind. My resolve to be alone started to waiver, and the longer I sat in silence, trapped within the sauna that was the truck cab, the weaker it got. Beads of sweat formed over my brow and began to trickle down the side of my face as I closed my eyes, hoping to block out the heat as I closed myself off to the rest of the world.

I'd all but decided to leave the truck and attempt to find my family in the long aisles of the grocery store when I felt my cell phone vibrate in my front pocket. I removed it and looked at its front LCD screen curiously. The number that was flashing across it had a Michigan area code. I didn't know anyone in Michigan who'd want to call me, and I usually don't answer calls from numbers that I don't recognize. The same impulse that had driven me to endure the insufferable truck cab rather than peruse the air – conditioned aisles of the store with my family made me want to answer this call. I couldn't explain why I wanted to be alone or why I wanted to answer this call, but I flipped the front screen of my phone up. Pressing it to my ear, I gave an uncertain, "Hello."

The baritone voice that came over the receiver was strange, unfamiliar to me as it gave a wary, initial, "Hey there," in return. Soon, though, all my doubts slipped away. "I've missed you, Meg," he said, his voice full of affection and longing. "Where have you been for the past year?"

When I heard those words, I instantly knew who it was, and I hoped that he could make everything okay again.

We crossed the bridge that goes over the kayak training course and wound our way through the various paths until we reached the river's edge. There was a set of seven or eight huge steps leading down to the water's surface. We descended them, stopping at the next to bottom step and sat down. I leaned against him, shivering involuntarily, despite the warm breeze. To anyone walking past us, we appeared to be the typical teenage couple. But appearances can be deceiving. I knew how much he cared about me, and I vividly recalled the first time he told me that he loved me. Yet he hadn't made any other attempts to further our relationship. He was my best friend, and I knew that he always would be.

We watched as the malodorous river water surged over the concrete waterfall. We talked about the horseshoe shape that the falls made, and the raw power that they portray. Off-white foam formed as the river widened away from the falls and the water was allowed to settle. The foam floated over the water and was eventually pushed to the edge of the river where it flowed along with the slower current. We watched as brightly colored leaves fell from the trees around us. Each leaf was caught by a different wind current, and each one danced its own, unique step. My attention was caught as some of the river foam floated past us, carrying the river's familiar pungent odor with it. I felt him shift as he tenderly wrapped his hand around mine. Interlacing our fingers, he took me by the hand for the first time. It was then that I undoubtedly knew that I loved him.

Not Yet Gone

Poetry by Audrey Mahank, Senior
Colored Pencil by Samantha Palmer, Junior

Money and miles, jobs and a car
finding a hell in this place so far
I'll miss your touch and the rush of your skin
but you'll hear my voice sway like the wind.

I love you here like I'll love you there
there's one thing we'll forever share
The stars are my eyes watching you cry
the rain is my presence always nearby.

Baby, I'm leaving but I'll always be near
watch the sky and I'll be here
Tears and coins, dimes and a goodbye
don't worry our love will withstand time.

Love will last the trials we face
our love will fill the empty space.
Baby, I'm leaving but I'll always be near
watch the sky and I'll be here.

Goodbye goodbye fate will seal my woes
goodbye goodbye I promise I'll be home
For the stars are your eyes watching me cry
the rain is your presence always nearby.

Ditsch Pretzels

Nonfiction by Lina Hennig, Junior, German Exchange Student
Watercolor by Garrett Blad, Senior

Currently, I'm in America. Everything is amazing, and the food is especially better than in Germany. However, there is one thing that no food in the world can replace for me. But that has a different background, a personal connection.

I was born in Suhl, a small city in the middle of Thuringia, a state in Germany. I lived with my parents and my brother in a wonderful house, next to the city. I loved every day there. I used to go to the city with my mom but not to buy toys or candy. Just going to the city and walking next to my mom was enough for me to enjoy the trips every week. In the middle of the city is a very small bakery which is called "Ditsch." The Ditsch pretzels were the one thing I always wanted. Every time I went to the city, I said, "MO-O-OM, can I ple-ease get a pretzel?" She started smiling and gave me the money. That was a great feeling for a 6 year old girl to buy her own pretzel.

The seller knew me, and she knew what I wanted – everyday. Every time I'd say, " A warm, very salty pretzel, please," and it would start my big smile. American readers need to know: We Germans eat our pretzels only with salt. Not with cheese or other dip. Only with salt, and I love that taste. The Ditsch pretzels are not very big, but the taste is so awesome, especially when they are hot. Also, I don't eat my pretzel slowly, although I do enjoy every second of this delicacy. It doesn't take but two minutes for eating the whole pretzel.

My dad and my brother often accompanied us. Those were happy family trips for me. My brother and I in the middle of our lovely parents. What a great feeling, and they were never without a pretzel either.

When I was 8 years old, my parents got divorced. My dad left our house and lived in an apartment in the same city. It was a "good" divorce. I never saw my parents in a fight or anything like that. We went to my dad's often. But over time, my mom met a new man, and we left the house, too. It was our house, built by my parents. So, my dad moved back in our original house, and we live 30 minutes by car away from him. Mom's new boyfriend is a good guy. He is lovely and nice, and I love the new city. I have all my friends there, and the school is better. I see my dad every second weekend.

My brother is no longer with my dad. He doesn't have time because of his work. I love my dad. I love the time in Suhl. We still go into the city often. In the meantime there is a new seller at the Ditsch bakery, but I still start every time with the same smile when I get my very warm, salted pretzel, and I always pay for it myself, even if it is with daddy's money.

I think I will always want a warm pretzel because the warmth reminds me of the love and comfortable feeling with my family. The salt? I have no idea why, but I love salt, and I eat nearly everything with salt. The best thing about Ditsch pretzels is the taste is always the same; I know these pretzels. And when I eat my pretzel, I always think about the comfortable feelings and the family time with both of my parents in Suhl. Sometimes I try to imagine what a kind of girl I would be if my parents wouldn't have divorced.

Ditsch pretzels are really my family's special treat in Suhl. While Ditsch bakeries are famous in Germany, they are all very small, nothing with sit-ins. The only thing you can do is grab your food and enjoy it on the way. I see these bakeries in many cities, but I never eat a Ditsch pretzel in any other city than Suhl. None from any other seller than "my" seller. I don't want to go other places with that warm feeling or without one of my parents. Ditsch pretzels are happiness for me.

(Translated into German by Lina)

Ditschbrezeln

Tatsachenbericht von Lina Hennig, 11. Klasse, Deutsche Austauschschülerin
Wasserfarbenbild von Garrett Blad, 12. Klasse

Momentan verbinge ich ein Jahr in Amerika. Es ist einfach genial und alles, besonders das Essen, ist besser als in Deutschland. Doch eine Sache fällt mir ein, dass kein Dessert oder Essen auf der Welt für mich ersetzen kann, aber das hat einen anderen Grund, eine persönliche Ansicht.

Ich bin in Suhl geboren, einer kleinen Stadt in Thüringen. Ich habe mit meinen Eltern und meinem Bruder in einem Stadthaus gewohnt. Jeder tag war etwas besonderes, Mama und ich sind fast täglich in die Stadt gegangen. Nicht um Süssigkeiten oder oder Spielzeug zu kaufen, einfach nur neben meiner Mama durch die Stadt zu gehen, hat mir jedes mal auf's neue ein unvergessliches Gefühl gegeben. In der Mitte unseres tägliches Spazierganges sind wir an einer Bäkerei namens "Ditsch" vorbei gekommenen. Eine Brezel von Ditsch war, was ich jedes mal wollte. Jedes mal wenn Ditsch in unserer Sichtweite war, fragte ich "MAAAMAAA- kann ich eine Brezel haben?" und sie hat jedes mal mit einem lächeln beobachtet, wie ich meine Brezel selber kaufe, nachdem sie mir Geld gegeben hatte. Mit 6 Jahren empfand ich es als ein unbeschreibliches Gefühl der Verkäuferin persönlich das Geld zu geben und meine Brezel selber zu bestellen.

Bei der Bäkerin war ich schon bekannt und sie wusste immer, was ich wollte, trotzdem hat sie sich jedes mal meine Bestellung angehört: „ Eine warme Brezel mit viel Salz, bitte" und mich familiär angelächelt. Denn was Amerikaner nicht wissen: Wir Deutschen essen unsere Brezeln nur mit Salz, nicht mit Käse oder einer Soße. Einfach nur Salz – und genau so liebe ich es. Ditschbrezeln sind nicht besonders groß, aber der Geschmack ist unglaublich, besonders wenn sie frisch aus dem Ofen sind. Deswegen esse ich meine Brezeln nie langsam, geniesse aber jeden Bissen und brauche nie länger als 2 Minuten für eine komplette Brezel.

Mein Bruder und mein Papa haben uns oft in die Stadt begleitet. Das waren die besten Familienausflüge für mich: Mein großer Bruder und ich zwischen unseren geliebten Eltern. Das gab mir immer ein wunderbares Gefühl, besonders wenn ich 4 Brezeln

bestellen konnte.

Als ich 8 Jahre alt war, haben sie meine Eltern scheiden lassen. Mein Vater ist ausgezogen und hat sich eine Wohnung in unserer Nähe gesucht. Meine Eltern haben sich weiterhin gut verstanden und wir haben unseren Papa sehr oft besucht. Doch mit der Zeit hat meine Mama einen neuen Mann kennen gelernt und auch wir haben das Haus verlassen – unser Haus, gebaut bei meinen Eltern. Zum Glück wohnt mein Vater jetzt wieder in dem Haus und wir brauchen nicht einmal 30 Minuten um ihn zu besuchen. Ich mag meinen Stiefvater sehr, er war von Anfang an lieb zu uns und ich mag die Stadt, in der wir jetzt wohnen. Alle meine Freunde wohnen da und ich gehe dort zur Schule. Ich verbringe jedes zweite Wochenende bei meinem Papa, leider ohne meinen Bruder, da der wegen seiner Arbeit keine Zeit findet. Ich liebe meinen Papa und die Zeit in Suhl, natürlich gehen wir immer in die Stadt. Es ist zwar ein anderer Verkäufer bei Ditsch, trotzdem bekomme ich jedes mal dieses heimische Gefühl und das selbe Lächeln, wenn ich meine warme, salzige Brezel bestelle und selber bezahle, wenn auch mit Papa's Geld.

Ich denke, der Grund, dass ich immer eine warme Brezel bestelle ist das die Wärme mich an das stolze und sichere Gefühl mit meiner Familie erinnert. Und das Salz? Keine Ahnung warum ich Salz so liebe, es gehört einfach dazu. Zum Glück schmecken Ditschbrezel immernoch genauso wie vor 10 Jahren und wenn ich meine Brezel dann esse, erinnere ich mich mit jedem Bissen an zurück an die wunderschöne Zeit mit meinen Eltern in Suhl. Manchmal denke ich darüber nach, was für ein Mädchen ich wäre, wenn sich meine Eltern nie scheiden lassen hätten. Wie ich aussehen würde, was für Freunde ich hätte und welche Suhler Schule ich wohl besuchen würde.

Also, Ditschbrezeln sind einfach mein Highlight in Suhl. Ditschbäkerein gibt es überall in Deutschland, alle sehr klein, niemals mit Sitzgelegenheiten. Das einzige was man machen kann ist sein Essen bestellen und es unterwegs geniessen. Egal wo - ein unbeschreiblicher Geschmack. Trotzdem esse ich meine Brezeln nirgendwo anders als in Suhl und ich brauche auch das Gefühl nicht, wenn ich nicht mit meinen Eltern unterwegs bin. Ditschbrezeln machen mich einfach glücklich und wecken alte Erinnerungen in mir. Und ich weiß, eine Brezel von Ditsch wird das erste sein, was ich esse, nachdem ich mein Jahr in Amerika abgeschlossen habe.

The *Christmas* Gift

Nonfiction by Adrienne Erickson, Senior
Pencil by James Bowen, Senior

During the Christmas season of '98, I was six years old. I don't remember much about my life at that point, but one memory will always stand out. I didn't realize it then, but my brief introduction to one woman would change my beliefs about humanity forever. Because of her, I believe in the power of selflessness.

It all started with a doll. A doll that had seen many tea parties and fashion shows, but had somehow been tucked into the corner of the closet and forgotten about. My mother brought her out one day and suggested that I donate her to another little girl. This little girl didn't have nice toys and things to play with like I did, my mother explained to me. She told me that the women in the OB unit at Saint Joseph's Regional Medical Center in Mishawaka, where she worked, had decided to adopt this little girl's family for Christmas and needed me to give up my old toys. I was reluctant at first, but my mom told me of families that were less fortunate than ours, and I knew I wanted to do what I could to help that little girl. Together, we gathered three large moving boxes full of toys and clothes I had outgrown.

The day came for us to deliver all the clothes, toys, food, and baby supplies that the entire OB unit had collected. I went with my mother and two other women from the unit. We drove to a run down neighborhood in South Bend, the likes of which I had never seen before. I was alarmed to see dilapidated houses, some vacant, overgrown weeds, and old, rusted cars parked along the sidewalk. The car stopped in front of a small white house, barely bigger than my kitchen, that the woman lived in with her four children. I didn't want to go in, but my mom and her friends walked me to the front door.

I don't know what I expected but what I saw changed me. A woman, slightly younger than my mother, answered the door in an old, baggy T-shirt. Her hair had been sloppily thrown into a bun on the side of her head, and she was holding a small boy on her hip. I peered into the cluttered house and saw that they were packed in tightly. There were two mattresses, a small dining table, and toys strewn about the room. She seemed surprised to see us and didn't know who we were or why we had shown up on her doorstep.

One of my mother's friends explained to her that for the past two weeks, her hospital unit had been collecting items to help make their Christmas brighter. I will never forget the woman's reaction as long as I live. She broke down sobbing and hugged all of us, squeezing us if she'd never let go, while apologizing for being too emotional. "God bless you," she kept repeating. "God bless you."

I was too young to fully understand the significance of what happened that day. When I look back on it now, I get a little choked up over that story. Something about it just gets to me, and I realized something very important, we are not here to simply peacefully coexist. We are here to serve others.

Finding You

Poetry by Nick Havranek, Junior
Charcoal by Olivia Hurley, Senior

You walked up to me with that strange
smile and took me by the hand
showed me a new way
made me forget this place
kept my mind in check
and took everything but the kitchen sink

As I watched my kingdom sink
I felt fine because I had you.
You made more sense than anything. I checked.
You kept my hands
warm and safe in this awful place.
Everything else just melted away.

The feeling could never be outweighed;
that heavy heart couldn't sink
anymore. How do you create this place?
Science could never explain it. It's normally strange.
We walked on the beach, hand-in-hand,
while avoiding a reality check.

Happiness was always on my list. Check
it off. We don't need them anyway.
Carefully slapped by society's cold hand
rebels alone together in this world, we sink
their ships and burn the bridges with strange
eyes and judging voices. We come in first place.

We make the most of every second in this place.
Later, we'll worry about that check.
You look at me and it all fades away. Strange
to think, but easy to see in that way.
We understand what we see in sync
and what is just secondhand.

Once cold and shivering hands
are now pure and in place.
Thanks to you, we won't sink
no matter what. It's a check
in the box of life, and the way
I feel is exotic and strange.

But those "strange" feelings no longer linger in my hands.
They have scattered away. They have left this place.
I've checked for a trace of you, as my heart sinks once more.

The Many Meanings of Etna Green

Poetry by Emily Thomas, Senior
Photo by Emily Thomas, Senior

The airport is a prison as it takes me far away from you...
Trapped and small. I need to see him again. I can't possibly be leaving! The last thing I want to be doing is boarding a plane back to reality. Back home...

The birds were meant for tears and this cabin full of fools...
Seagulls followed the cruise ship when we left Sicily. His town. I watched Palermo fade into the distance, until it was just a mass of land, until I had to go back to the stateroom. Alone in the familiarity of my family...

I'll set my songs to shuffle as I'm reminded how the miles pass over each green and golden field...
This ridiculous distance is killing me. I turn up 'Parachute,' the acoustic version, like I did when I crossed over the endless fields of green and gold, a patchwork quilt to my little journey, a journey that is ending. I'm in the airport now. There are only memories left...

As small talk reaches ear, I find myself remembering all these things I left behind...
I was submerged headfirst in culture and language. They all spoke Italian, all except for my Davide. I felt so angry at myself for not being able to understand them. If only I had learned a few words before I left...

And I know its cold outside, I can tell by the frost. But what I wouldn't do for a parachute....
It was cold the night he upset me, as I paced on the top deck, wind rushing through my hair, as I cried silently. A few tears fell to the warm waters below, into the Mediterranean, as I leaned over the guard rail. If I fell, no one would even know. What I wouldn't do for a parachute...

Take back the time we knew. We used to run away, run away with ourselves, only guiding ourselves...
I wanted to leave him at first, to never see those brown eyes again. I could never be sure, when I was with him. We were lost, wandering until things made sense. Or at least I was...

So do this one more time, take my hand. Only one more time. I'll give you one last chance to make it right...
We were tossed together again, on the last night I ever saw him...

And as hours pass, miles grow distant and I think of how I left you there...
In time we grew closer to being apart, in a strange moment of (red blooded? American?) impulsiveness, I kissed him, in an elevator full of people, as the night grew old and wise. Then I ran...

This isn't better for me, is this better for you? Because it's still so cold outside. And I can't be alone tonight....
I never looked back, and he never called my name...

I can't be alone tonight...
I can't be alone tonight....

My city sleeps in agony without you. Walking all the streets that we once took and made our home...
The hallways are empty, then again it is late. I stumble over my feet. I'm clumsy in my dancing dress and high heels...

And I drive all night to hold you just for one second more. I'm down with anything you want from me and more....
I stayed up the next night to forget him. I danced for him. I danced to forget....

'Cause as small talk reaches ear, I find myself remembering all these things I left behind...
The Italian irks me: "Americano," "Emily and Davide," "Bacio." I can hear the heavy connotations in their voices. I wish I could talk to my friends back home...

This isn't better for me. Is this better for you? Well, 'cause it's still so cold outside...
I'm alone now...

You know I cant' be alone tonight. Don't you know I can't be alone tonight....
What can I do?...

'Cause all these miles in between, kid, you know it's you and me. And I can't be alone tonight...
America and Italy, that's how it is now. Unless...

So can we drive? We can beat this hellish cold with our pedal to the floor. Close your eyes....
I run off, totally leaving my parents and my brother. I hail a cab and throw Euros in the driver's lap. "Palermo! Palermo!" We drive. I board a small boat. In no time, I am at the fountain where I last saw him, where I hadn't had the courage to speak to him for one last time. Maybe, just maybe...

Let this pavement guide you home to the place we are still together...
I arrive to see a brown skinned boy with chocolate eyes and a smile to melt my uncertainties, waiting for me.

It's almost midnight and four friends, Charlie, Raven, Miley, and Summer are sitting in Miley's room. It's almost midnight and Raven is trying to sleep while the other girls sit up in their pajamas talking. They are all 15.

Miley: Hey! Let's play a game!

Summer: (excited) Yeah! What game though?

Post WEDDING Jitters

Miley: How about hide-and-seek?

Charlie: hide-and-seek? What are we? 10?

Summer: How about we play (slight pause then creepy smile) truth or dare?

The other girls look at each other with excitement as Raven covers her ears with a pillow.

Charlie: Ay! Raven, wake up! We're gonna play truth or dare. You're gonna miss it!

Raven: (muffled) I don't care! Let me sleep in peace!

Miley: Come on! You always say that you don't want to play and then you have so much fun. Let's just play for, like, ten minutes, and if you're still not having fun, you can go back to sleep. K?

Raven: (takes pillow off of her face and throws it across the bed) Fine! Ten minutes. That's it. Then I'm going to sleep. (she gets up and joins the other girls on the floor)

Summer: Okay. Who wants to go first?

Charlie: Me! I will! Raven, truth (whispered in a scary voice) or dare?

Raven: Really? You're gonna pick me first?

Charlie: Shut up and pick one.

Raven: (rolls eyes) Whatever. Dare.

Charlie: I dare you to hmmmmm (She ponders for a while while glancing around the room.)

(She stands up suddenly and runs out

Drama by Nick Havranek, Junior Pencil by Blake Harris, Senior

of the room)

Miley: Ummm. Where is she going?

Raven: I have no idea. Was that my dare?

(Then Charlie bursts back into the room, holding a beautiful white wedding dress)

Charlie: I dare you to put this on and run down the street while yelling, "I'm brinin' sexy back," over and over again.

Miley: Charlie, put that back! That's my mom's!

Charlie: Relax. She's not even home. She'll never know. (Charlie throws the dress at Raven.)

Raven: I don't know. If Miley doesn't want us to...

Charlie: Miley is a freaking baby. Just do it. I dared you!

Raven: (Looks at Miley for some sign of defiance in her, but Miley doesn't seem to care.) Fine.

(Charlie smiles and jumps out the door with the other girls following closely behind.)

(They approach the front door and Raven slips the dress over her head and slides her arms in the armholes.)

Raven: It's a little long. (Raven grabs the sides of the dress and lifts them so the dress isn't dragging on the ground.)

Charlie: Come on! Go! (Charlie opens the front door and starts pushing Raven out)

Miley: (shouting to Raven) Be careful!

Raven: Stop pushing me, Charlie!

(Charlie let go of Raven and ran back to the door, leaving Raven by the road. The sky was pitch black, and she could only see a lone street light in the distance. She started running down to the opposite end of the street and stood still. She promptly turned around to face the girls.)

Raven: (skipping down the street) I'm bringing sexy back! Yeah!

(Suddenly, she heard thunder and a flash of lightening filled the sky. Raven screamed)

Miley: (Whispering to herself) Oh no. (Shouting to Raven out the door) Run! Hurry, Raven! Run!

(Then the rain starts pouring down on Raven and on the dress. She flings her arms into the air and tries to cover the dress in vain)

Raven: (muttering to herself) No. no. no. no. no. no. no. no. (She trips in the street and splashes the dress with a nice helping of muddy water)(yelling) Damn!

(The other girls all gasp.)

Miley: No! Get in here now!

(Charlie backs into the house first, and the others follow.)(They all sit in the living room on the couch as Raven and Miley hold the dress in their laps)

Summer: Nice job, Charlie!

Charlie: How was that my fault?

Summer: How was that not your fault?

Charlie: How was I supposed to know it was gonna rain? I'm not a freaking weather girl!

Raven: If you hadn't dared me to do this, none of this would've happened!

Charlie: But Miley was the one who convinced you to play. None of this would've happened if she didn't wake you up.

Miley: Summer was the one who wanted to play Truth or Dare! None of this would've happened if she just

would've played hide-and-seek.

Summer: Do NOT try to blame this on me! I'm not the one who decided to go outside in her friend's mom's wedding dress.

Miley: This isn't getting us anywhere. Let's just calm down and think. How con we get the stains out?

Charlie: We could put it in the washing machine.

Miley: Are you stupid? It'll shrink or something!

Charlie: Nu-uh! That only happens in the movies, moron.

Miley: We're not gonna chance it.

Charlie: Fine. Don't listen to me.

Miley: Fine! I won't. (pauses to calm down) Anyone else have any ideas?

(Raven and Summer look at each other and shrug. Miley sighs.)

Miley: Whatever. Let's put it in the wash.

(The lights go down and when the lights go back on, we are in the laundry room waiting for the dress to finish.)

Summer: How much longer?

(Timer goes off on the washing machine)

Miley: Oh! It's done!

(Miley pulls out the dress to see all of its tears and that it had shrunk)

Miley: So it only happens in movies, huh?

Raven: Are we still having fun,

Charlie?

Charlie: Would you two just shut up. We can fix this!

Summer: How? How could we possibly fix this dress? Tell me! I'd love to know.

Charlie: (glaring at Summer) I don't know! Just do something! Bury it in the backyard! I don't care!

(Charlie walks out of the room and everyone is silent.)

Miley: That's not a bad idea.

Summer: You can't be serious.

Miley: Well, it's not like my mom would ever go looking for it anyway. If it's buried in the ground, she'll just think the dog buried it.

Raven: Wow. I'm out. (Raven leaves the room to join Charlie.)

Miley: Fine! Leave! I don't care! Summer and I can do this alone. Right, Summer?

Summer: Ummm, actually, I think I'm gonna sit this one out, too. (She leaves also)

Miley: You're all no longer my friends! Just go home! (Miley drags the dress out the door.)

(*The light goes down and when it comes back up, we see Miley in the backyard with a shovel and the dress. She has begun digging a somewhat large hole.*)

Miley: (mumbling to herself) Stupid dress. Stupid truth or dare.

(Suddenly there's a flash of light on Miley and an unknown voice is heard.)

Charcoal by Kim Lord, Junior

???: Miley? What are you doing?

Miley: Who's there?

???: Is that my dress? What happened? What are you doing?

Miley: Mom? Oh no! No! No! What are you doing home?

Miley's mom: I caught the red eye home. What are YOU doing?

Miley: Ummm, well. (She starts rushing her words in a panic.) Raven wanted to sleep but we were all awake and talking, then someone got the idea to play truth or dare and I didn't want to, but we did anyway, and Charlie dared Raven to wear your dress outside while singing, "I'm bringing sexy back," and I told her not to, but she did anyway, and it started raining and and... (She bursts into tears and drops the shovel and falls to the ground.) I just wanted to fix it! (crying like a baby at this point)

Miley's mom: Honey! Honey. Calm down. (She kneels down and hugs Miley.) It's ok! That dress is only a dress. I have you and your father to show me what's important in life. And I thank God for that every day.

Miley: So, you're not mad? (Sniffling)

Miley: No, sweetheart. (She stands up with Miley, and they start walking back to the house) But you're grounded until your wedding day.

End.

Forever My Summer

Poetry by Emily Thomas, Senior
Colored Pencil by Anna Schmalzried, Junior

Scream.
I dare you.
Sunroof down, with the summer air whipping your carrot-top-goldie locks
every which way,
just let go,
as you sing along to every song you know on the radio
and fall into the bathwater-warm Indiana ocean,
the sand between your toes, the sky glittering with diamonds.
Laugh, Darling!
Your sweet face lights up more than the city lights,
more than the skyline,
more than the Ferris wheel,
when we spilt candy apples with candy coated grins. It was a kiss-on-the-cheek sort of feeling,
like at the drive-in, where I giggled at the thought of spending time alone.
As the fireworks go off, be mesmerized.
Your eyes come so close to making me as dizzy as a somersault- cartwheel,
hand springing good time.
Dance with me dear, spin with the earth.
Touch the sky- it's easy on a rooftop-braving the roughness of your hands and your curves.
You inspire me.
I only hope that the butterflies in my heart don't escape when I laugh at the storm,
thunder, lightning, candles.
Green eyes and blue, next to a pitcher of lemonade-
Isn't the world such a beautiful place?
I feel so alive with you, I am so ...free.
If I could fly, I would.
I'd fly with the moon across the sky to my better place:
The night that we lay abandoned in the street as you leaned in close and
whispered, "Will you be my forever?"
So,
I scream
as happiness
envelops
me
and you put the ring on my hand.
Slow my trembling heart, darling,
and keep me here in this bliss
forever.
Forever in this moment
forever, my summer.

Summer Sestina

Poetry by Emily Thomas, Senior
Tempra by Anna Schmalzried, Junior

A place of refuge in a summer rainstorm. Home.
As I walk through the woods, a free
bird flying with a friend, I smile,
for I dare to flutter to a long stretching tree limb, flying,
with daring
demeanors, as the sunlight

filters through the leaves. Sunlight
is my home.
I walk with my darling
as we talk about simple things, free
of concerns. He watches the shadows on my face and I fly.
As he catches my eyes, I catch his imperfect smile.

We talk until the wee hours of morning, a new day smiling
with sunlight
upon our faces. I wish he wouldn't leave. The lazy buzzing flies
and summertime noises startle me as fireworks erupt. My home
is welcome, yet my life is vulnerable, freely
spinning out of control, except for my darling.

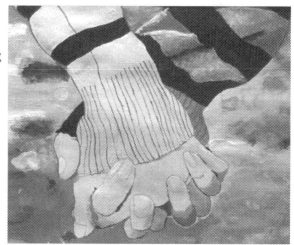

His little sister with blonde hair and lion eyes stares, daring
me to not smile.
His parents talk of freedom
and childhood, as I sit at a kitchen table, the sunlight
making shimmering spirals in a whimsical way. His home,
his life, fly

away from me for a moment. The months fly
by and I forget about his face and his daring
eyes hiding a place in life for me. A home
with a smile
and pure sweet lies made of sunlight
and freedom

to forget. And as freely
as I lost him in my mind, he haunts me again with his crooked smile
and sunlight
persona. He meets me in the morning, out of the blue sky. My darling.
We soar for awhile in a child's mile
as I try to find my way home.

He is really sort of a lovely thing, full of homely,
warmth, bright eyes and free
laughter. He makes me smile,
makes me fly,
my darling songbird, my darling.
Perhaps, in the future, we will walk together again in the sunlight.

I Don't Mind

Poetry by Emily Thomas, Senior
Pastel by Garrett Blad, Senior
Scholastic Art Award Gold Key

Write me a letter in the words of blue denim,

with the wind and the shade trees highlighting

that watermelon smile.

Pour me a cup of kindness in the form of a new dance,

when the rain clouds wash out my green eyes,

as I spin like a child.

I'd sit in a rocking chair on my front porch,

lemonade in hand,

counting the stars in the sky and

the headlights on the highway.

I'd sneak out my window and jump into your arms

and just

stay, as though we had all night long.

The phone rings as I sing in my kitchen

and I can't wait to be with you.

We talk. And don't stop, kid, you're too

amazing

not to deserve everything; you deserve everything.

You're a strange one, I know,

but as I lean in closer and look at that

perfectly imperfect face,

I realize that I don't mind.

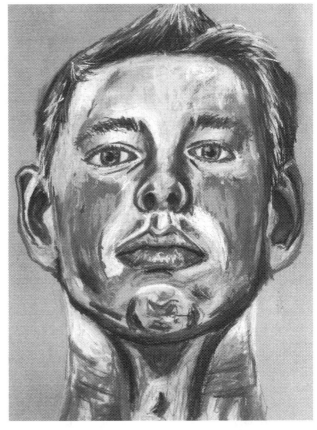

When I was on vacation this past summer, my aunt Beth, my father's sister, called me into her room after a family dinner. As I stared at this woman, I felt as if we were strangers. Too far away from each other to truly know one another, grief and sadness keeping her from me. As her eyes started to fill with tears, I noticed there was something in a large black trash bag laying on her neatly made bed. In an effort to hide her tears, she turned to it, noisily wiping her nose and eyes on the sleeve of her shirt. As she spoke, her voice startled me. It wasn't her smooth velvet voice with the hint of southern twang. It was rough and out of pitch from trying to hold back her tears. She sat on her bed and motioned for me to join her. As soon as I did, my eyes started to itch, and tears began flowing from my eyes.

We looked at each other, and without saying a word, we both simultaneously broke into laughter. Through sniffles and giggles, she started talking to me. She apologized to me, which at first confused me. She had done nothing to me; she had never wronged me. I'm not sure, but I think my face gave my confusion away, and so she explained. "Danielle," she said, " you are going to be 18 years old on March 26th. I only remember because you are just two days older than Joe, and I am sorry for not ever saying I love you." When I tried to interrupt to inform her, she just held up a hand. "I may have said it a few times," she continued, "but not ever enough, and we never visit. That is a trend that will soon be stopping." The next few words that she spoke brought me to tears again, and my cries were followed with hiccups because they lasted for a long time. "Danielle, seeing you, your mom, and your sisters so happy and well makes me angry. Angry because my brother doesn't get to see it. He left you, and he missed it all. But I have a gift for you. I know he would've wanted you to have it."

She turned her back to me and rustled the coat from the bag. Oh, the smell. It filled my nostrils as soon as it was free from the bag. I despise leather. The smell makes my stomach turn. The feeling makes my skin crawl. I would never touch it, but what could I tell her? As she hung the coat over my dangling legs, a shiver erupted through my body. "This was Richard's, your dad's. He got it for Christmas not long before they moved down here to Texas. Oh, how he loved this jacket." I didn't know what to say. My lips seemed frozen, unable to say anything. My shirt was getting damp because I couldn't stop my tears. At that moment, I was closer to my father than ever before.

My aunt kissed me on the forehead and left the room, knowing that all I needed was space and time to clear my fogged mind. I looked at the jacket, its black color faded with time. The leather was worn down in some spots. I felt it. The texture was unlike any leather that I've felt before. My mind wandered to a photo in an old album that was tucked in a shelf back home. My father, young in years, smiling, wearing the dreadful coat.

I held the jacket, at first far from my body, then as I became accustomed to the idea, I pulled it closer. My fingers glided over the old material, and they soon found a pocket. I unbuttoned the clasp and plunged my hand deep into the hidden space. *Silk? Is that what I am feeling,* I thought. It seemed so strange that such an ugly, manly jacket was lined with a cloth

the Jacket

so...feminine. I closed my eyes picturing all the items that my lost father once stowed away in this pocket. I placed the jacket on its back, soaking in the image. It seemed such a drastic picture. Faded black outside, canary yellow lining. Without thinking I put my arms in the oversized sleeves. I tried to zip the jacket, but the zipper had been unmoved in so many years, trying to move it was a fruitless. I curled up on the bed, wrapping my arms around myself tightly, physically and emotionally drained. I let my heavy eyelids droop, and I fell into a deep slumber. When I awoke, the jacket was back in the bag, and I was covered in a blanket.

My father's jacket remains in the black trash bag, hidden deep in our linen closet. Sometimes, when no one is home, I dig out the bag and pull out the jacket. I let my fingers wander over the pockets and collar, and every time I do, I seem to create new images of my father. My jacket is not with me all the time, but it is still something deeply personal. It's the only intimate piece that I have of my father, and that's why it's so perfect.

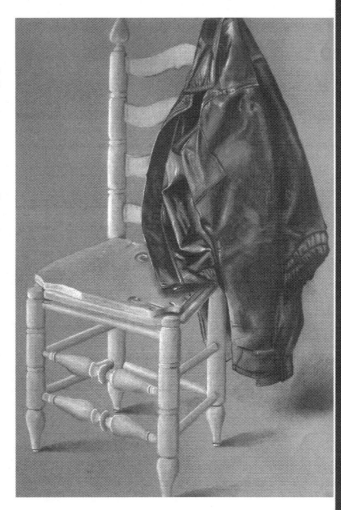

Nonfiction by Danielle Wolfe, Senior

Charcoal by Garrett Blad, Senior

Scholastic Art Award Silver Key

Story of John Sloan's Traveling Carnival Santa Fe

Poem by Emily Thomas, Senior
Scholastic Writing Award Gold Key
Charcoal by Hannah Bottorff, Sophomore

They walk about in the moonlight

With a rosy glow setting off the shadows in a small girl's face.

She walks with another, whispering in her ear,

A clear night in Santa Fe.

A cowboy and a lady in blue,

With a broad hat and a string of pearls,

Smiling at the children on the carousel,

A clear night in Santa Fe.

Women wearing habits,

Rosaries in hand they walk along

At peace in the heavy air,

A clear night in Santa Fe.

The crowd licks at the feet of a Ferris wheel

Lit up like a candle,

The flame the lights, the flame the people,

A clear night in Santa Fe.

The world spins as I continue

To ride the white horse,

My pink dress billowing out,

As I sit backwards, a little rebel.

Watch me reach for the brass ring.

I could catch it any day

On a clear night in Santa Fe.

She Is

Poetry by Matt Philson, Junior
Photo by Kate Smith, Senior

She is the smell of fresh air
She is the smoke from
a fire that burns forever
She is the mirror that
reflects the one she loves
She is the rose
that never dies, never changes colors
She's the heartbeat
of a child
the one who chills out
in the cold
the one that breathes
those few words
I love you
She is the constant rain
that never stops
She's the summer
that never ends
She's the one who stays by your side
She's the constant
dripping of water waiting
to be collected
the pile of dirt waiting to be picked up
a broken piece of metal
waiting to be mended
and made new
She is the
constant dripping
of water

MAGNIFICENT MIRANDA

I am in love with a comic book character because it won't get me into trouble and real men have been too painful. Being the 22 year old, successful, independent woman that I am, that sounds completely deranged. However, in my short life, I've discovered that the men in my life have a tendency to walk out more often than not. They develop a bond with me that keeps me holding on, and than they disappear as if the wind just took them away.

Powerful Jimmy, the character of my dreams, is perfection waiting to burst out of the pages. He's so handsome; dark brown hair, muscular, strong, piercing blue eyes, a darker complexion (similar to a beach tan), compassionate, strong-willed, and of course, powerful. His ambition, to be the hero that he is, would just take your breath away. It certainly took my breath away.

Anyway, the story of this odd fantasy began when my last boyfriend, Greg, left me. We'd been together for two years, and then one day, he just never came back to our apartment. I was up late, worried sick, but he never came home. I tried calling his cell phone a million times, but there was no answer. A couple of days later, Greg came back to the apartment while I was at work, packed up all of his things, and left me a note in a half-empty apartment that said this:

Dear Lindsey,
I know that this wasn't supposed to happen, and I promise that I never meant for it to, but I met someone else. I love you, I do, but I needed something new. I'm so sorry for everything, but this is where it ends. I packed up all of my stuff and left. The key is on the bed. Again, I'm sorry for dropping this on you.
Greg

Ever since that day, I've felt such hatred towards men. I mean, how could someone who really loves you just up and leave like that? So, I've now decided that my life is not going to be about a man who will just disappoint me like Greg did. My life is going to be about me; working, relaxing, pulling myself together, and not spending any more of my time on worthless men. I suppose that's where Powerful Jimmy comes in.

Walking down 4th Street, there's a newspaper stand that I always glance at. They have magazines, comic books, newspapers, TV guides, and all of the newest, detailed reports on celebrity lives. On this particular day, I decided to pick up a comic book, *The Powerful Jimmy Series*, just to glance through it and laugh at the childlike quotations and illustrations. However, it pulled me in. Powerful Jimmy is the most amazing human being ever written about. All right, he may be fictional, but all the same, I think that I'm in love.

Whenever I feel upset about work or anything, I just pull out my new collection of *The Powerful Jimmy Series* and read my tears away. I know that it may sound completely crazy, but just simply reading those comic books makes me happy. The security of a superhero appearing out of nowhere whenever there's a crisis brings comfort to me.

POWERFUL JIMMY

Fiction by Autumn Ladyga, Senior
Ink by Mariah Rippy and Kirsten Brown, Juniors

[[*Creative Sparks*]]

Imagining Powerful Jimmy in my mind, I can only hope that someday, whether this be tomorrow or five years from now, someone identical to Powerful Jimmy will fly into my life.

Just two months later, I was out at a bar with my three best friends, Katie, Jewel, and Krystal, when my eyes focused on a man sitting on the complete opposite side of the bar. He didn't look like Powerful Jimmy or anything, but for some reason, my eyes couldn't stop dancing over in his direction. I assumed that he saw me as he began to make his way over to our table.

Really, I don't know what to tell you about what happened next. To put it bluntly, I realized that he was a dud just like the rest. After going on three dates, I knew that he wasn't what I was looking for. His mannerisms disgusted me; the way that he would talk to me with his mouth half-full and the way that he'd stare at his food more than at me. Being the neat freak that I am, it's needless to say that Bar Guy just wasn't my type.

After catapulting him from my life, I needed to really get a hold on reality. I started to question what I found so appealing

it his looks? Yes. Was it his strength? God, yes. Was it his consistency of being there through everything? Hell yes. More than anything, I was in love with the comic book character because of his faithfulness to stick

around. This might sound weird, but that characteristic made this fictional super hero so sexy to me. Why didn't he exist in real life? Are there any men out there that resemble him in any way, shape, or form?

For the remainder of that year, I stayed happily single. I threw away all of

could stop the cycle of disappointment that I was just putting upon myself. Finding a man was no longer important to me anymore, because I had come to the realization that making a list and ranking every man the

same just wasn't fair. Plus, all of the men that I encountered after putting a halt to the bar scene were just my co-workers. That just wasn't going to happen.

About a year later, I was walking past that same newspaper stand on 4th Street. I giggled to myself when I saw a new comic book series called *The Magnificent Miranda*

skimmed through it. The comic book series was about the strength and independence of Magnificent Miranda and how she made things happen in her own life.

Seeing this right before my eyes reminded me of how I had been just a year ago; lonely by choice. Being so picky had gotten the best of me and it took me so long to realize it. After purchasing the comic book, which I determined was going to be my new obsession, I went to the nearest coffee shop to get a mocha coffee and to fully examine the book. Do you know what happened? I met a guy. A terrific guy.

Seven months later, I was engaged to be married. I can not begin to tell you how random and strange this whole journey has been. In the end, I discovered the inner "Magnificent Miranda" in me. Along the way, I guess that I was just bound to meet my own "Powerful Jimmy" to make me complete. Now I know that he wants to be here and that he'll be here to save me if I'm ever a damsel in distress.

On Eagle's Wings

Poetry by Rachel Simms, Senior
Watercolor by Catrina Kroeger, Senior

I pour my soul into the rising melody,
Love lending strength to my faltering voice.

In every note, I see your face;
Before each pause, the light in your eyes.

Within my mind, your embrace awaits,
At the end of my song, running to your touch.

The crows can feel it, they simply know.
Forever yours, my heart shows through.

But they don't see, no others can feel
The music inside, with you as my muse.

No more need I write, never felt more true.
One was made for me, thus He gave me you.

In praise I lift my joy, my life,
That on eagle's wings, our song may rise.

Fragile Heart

Poetry by Kirsten Brown, Junior
Scholastic Writing Award Gold Key
Photo by Karen Celmer, Senior

Beads of water run down my cold glass
While I listen intently and wait for
The reason I came to this quiet place.
I am done with being alone
And I hope things stay turned around,
Even if for just one second.

I feel my body shiver the second
He walks through that old, glass
Door and begins to look around.
Immediately I forget what I'm here for
And can see him and him alone.
He always takes me to an exquisite place.

As he heads my way, I place
My hands on the second
Drink, so I don't have to drink alone.
He gratefully takes the refreshing glass
And we discuss what's best for
Us, with a bit of clowning around.

Birds gracefully fly around
This enchanted, changing place.
Whenever I'm here for
him, this derelict place changes in seconds.
Our hearts are fragile like glass,
But we don't have to tough it alone.

If he was to leave me alone,
I couldn't bring my thoughts around.
My life would shatter like glass,
But in my heart is a special place
Where I cherish each second
Like never before.

Even as young as four,
I couldn't stand to be alone.
Now he is my second
Heart, beating for this round
Earth, creating this glorious place.
I watch my life through a looking glass.

I view my glass life for
Placing me where I'm not alone,
Placing me around my heart, my every second.

Purple

Poetry by Autumn Ladyga, Senior
Charcoal by Garrett Blad, Senior

My midnight sky
on a warm summer's night
approaches with
the scent of
lavender Lenten candles
that make a room
glow and
show wondrous
potential and admiration,
while I swim
in my adventurous
night tales
and collaborative
purple out comings.

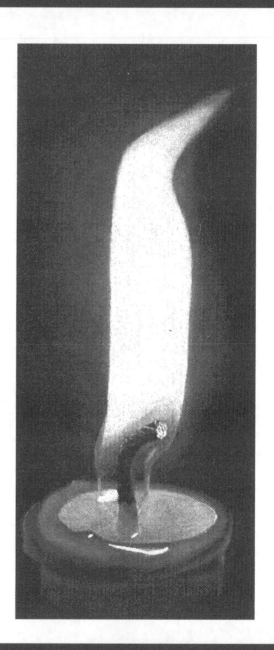

Don't Speak

Poetry by Chantell Cooper, Junior
Watercolor by Garrett Blad, Senior
Scholastic Art Award Gold Key

Don't speak
Never a word
A wish
A wish
For this to work
Words so simple
Never spoken.
A want
A dream
For such things to come
Just tell
Just let it be
Let it be
Never speak.
Simply stand by
Let happiness come to others
Let it be
Let it be
A want
A wish
For this to work.
Don't speak
Never a word

GRANDMA'S PHONE

Nonfiction by Kelsey Mitschelen, Senior
Scholastic Writing Gold Key Award
Charcoal by Meredith Rogers, Junior

The taste of stale potato chips still lingers in my mouth today. I could always count on my great-grandma Clark to have sour cream and onion flavored chips that were months past their expiration date. To her, they were still good; they just had an extra crisp. Another food she always had was Keebler cookies. They are the kind that are shaped like elves and have their names and comical sayings on the back. Those cookies were my favorite; she would take them out of the freezer and set them on the table in the middle of everyone for them to enjoy freely. I am still not sure why she kept them in the freezer; maybe to keep them fresh, I don't know why she worried about the cookies going bad and not the chips. Their frozen state never mattered much because we would all devour them before they even had a chance to thaw. But more than the food she had, I remember playing with my cousins. Every Thursday my whole family and I would make food and bring it to her house to visit and eat with everyone. We did this for years; ever since I can remember, this was a tradition.

Grandma Clark was tiny and brittle. It looked like she might break under gravity's strength. She always wore long dresses that she made from scratch; they flowed over her like a sheet that hid as much of her skin as possible. Most of her dresses contained some kind of floral pattern, which I assumed was common during her time. In her free time she would crochet blankets that were made from bright stripes of random colors repeated over and over again. But no matter what she was doing or who was visiting her she made sure she didn't miss her favorite T.V. show: Jeopardy.

Her house was as old as she was. I faintly remember seeing a picture of her house in a textbook at school; it had dinosaurs roaming around it ignoring the house, like it was there even before they were. It was white with a wire fence that surrounded her back yard. Her garage was ancient and scary. Its dark corners always scared me. I never knew what was going to crawl out of there, grab me and drag me back to its home to feast on me. Her car, a dark blue 1988 Sunbird, sat there begging to be driven. It was always parked in the garage and therefore had a gloomy look to it too. I never would have guessed that this car would become my first car. A car representing freedom for a young sixteen year old. The garage roof was low, and whenever we kids played hide and seek, it was the perfect place for the "big kids" to hide. I was too small to climb up there, so we younger children would look for them for hours. When we finally found them they would jump off the roof, jump over the fence, and take off running into the creepy woods in the back of her property. I have many memories there; many containing intense games of hide and seek, but my most vivid memory was when I was six.

I could hardly see the road in front of us. I was sitting in the sunken seat of our huge truck. The truck was a blue that always reminded me of the sky on a clear day. Its old doors squealed like mice whenever they were opened. The trucks roar as my mom increased the pressure of her foot on the pedal was a background for most of my childhood memories. To this day I still call it the "Pick 'Em Up Truck." I'm not quite sure why I called it that; maybe I just misunderstood my parents when they told us to climb in the pickup truck. I would look up and out the window. I could only see the light poles as we passed them. The sky behind them was a light blue, like the ones in the cartoons that seemed to be perfect all the time. The smell of freshly baked casserole floated through me, tricking my stomach and making it growl at me.

Those trips to her house seemed to take hours. I know it's not, but the anticipation in me would grow too strong to keep hidden. Before we could even pull into her driveway, I was unbuckled and ready to break through the truck's door. Her driveway was always filled to the max with relatives and their cars. As soon as my mom put the truck in park, I ripped the door open and sprinted towards the back door. I would fling her fence gate open and bash through the porch's screened door like superman on a mission to save someone's life.

There I would be met face-to-face with my cousin Taylor. He was a few years younger than me, but we were inseparable. His flaming red hair was always nice and cut short while my long, pale white hair was disheveled and thrown into a sloppy ponytail. To this day we are very different, but yet we got along so well. We almost collided as he came to meet me at the door. The huge smile on his face matched mine. We bolted further into her house and dashed down the stairs into the basement. It was like a lair for a vicious monster. I swear it lived in the old coal bin that sat in the front of the house. The coal bin was this little room that was filled with model airplanes and military mementos from my great-uncles but was always covered by an old shower curtain. We slowly walked through the first room that held the stairs. To the right were two old freezers that didn't work. Both were stuffed to the max with Avon products from the days when Great-Grandma Clark was an Avon sales lady. To the left were her old-fashioned washer and dryer that held no concern for us. The next room was always dark. It had a small toy box with random toys in it. The most memorable items she had in the box were an old, pink, hollow cat. The head of the cat had a chunk of plastic missing, but it still had sand in it. There was an old cigar box from my great aunt's childhood that had raw macaroni glued to it. Next to the toy box was a strawberry shortcake doll house that looked as if caveman played with it during their childhood.

On one of the tables that was closest to the coal bin sat two old fashioned telephones. The phones were the kind that when you wanted to call someone, you had to spin the small dial. The phones hadn't work in years but didn't have a speck of dust on them, unlike everything else around them. We scurried up to the phones and each grabbed one. Firmly holding the phones in our hands, we ran back up the old wooden stairs and onto the screened-in porch. There was a table in the middle, and two old yellow chairs sat each end of the table. The chairs were cracked from being used so much, but each slice in the plastic of the chairs was repaired with our family's favorite quick fix item: duct tape. Taylor and I would grab the two chairs and slide them closer to each other. We would set the phones on the table in front of us, look at each other and smile.

I looked back at the phone and began making a ringing noise with my mouth. Soon, Taylor started making the same noise. I'd reach for the receiver of my phone and hold it to my ear. The phone wasn't plugged in, so no sound came from it; no one would be talking on the other end. But my imagination took hold. Soon, I was having an interesting conversation with a person in a different country. I would laugh and continue our conversation. We both would hang up our phones, and seconds later, I would begin making the ringing noise again, imitating the sound that a working phone might make. I picked up the phone and said, "Hello." I imagined someone on the other end asking for Taylor. "Oh sure. He's right here," I would say and quickly hand the phone to Taylor and tell him that someone was asking to talk to him. Except Taylor was already pretending to talk to someone on his own dial phone. He would take my receiver anyways and try to juggle both of them, holding one to each ear. He would attempt to talk into both telephones, and I would start giggling hysterically. For some strange reason, this was the funniest thing to me, and at the sound of my laughter, Taylor would start laughing, too. We would play with those phones for hours.

The sky began to grow dark around us and our parents would walk up to us smiling at our laughter and childlike actions. With their commands still fresh in our minds, we would take the phones back down to the basement. The table that we found them on had two squares where the dust hadn't settled. We tried to put the phones directly in those two squares, placing them right where they have been for the past few months, maybe years. We galloped back upstairs and grabbed one last cookie. Climbing back into the "Pick 'Em Up Truck," I'd look back and wave at all my relatives leaving. I would begin questioning where the day had gone so quickly.

Twelve years later, Grandma Clark is gone. Cancer consumed her a few years ago. Sad days followed her death but now she is just a faint memory to me. I now go to school with Taylor; I'm a senior, and he's a junior. I don't talk to him anymore; we grew apart with age. I still wonder what happened to those two inseparable kids who were always playing with two old fashioned phones at Great-Grandma Clark's house. Whenever I see him walking with his friends in the school hallways laughing and pushing them around jokingly, I think back to those days. Long days of playing telephone with him, giggling and smiling. Simpler days. Every once in awhile he looks up and sees me looking directly at him. Faint smiles cross our faces, but we still part different hallways, different friends, different lives. As I walk with my friends, their conversation of the evil teachers' homework assignments becomes foggy in my mind. I wonder if he remembers those days, too. I grow sad knowing I'm not that close with him anymore. Maybe someday in the future that will change, and I will become best friends with my little cousin once again. Maybe I just need to give him a call on "our phones."

Innocent

Poetry by Emily Thomas, Senior
Scholastic Writing Gold Key Award
Watercolor by Amanda Bachtel, Senior

Train bells shake with might
When you taste like poetry.
Tongues of fire make a fight
Under whimsical starlight.
You are you because of me.
The fallout sends me under
Because of your trailing eyes.
Voice of reason, song of thunder,
Spellbound stare, I surrender.
All tied up in a lyrical lie,
A patchwork quilt ripped in places
As my dancing heart
Flutters, stutters, skips some places.
Old friends, new faces
Together and apart,
My voice catches in my throat
As we bask in the time
Before the door of youth drifts closed.
I know I will be fine.
Your breath is hot on the back of my neck
Spooking me a little, surprising me.
"Wanna run?" you ask with a grin.
I grab your hand and you reel me in.
We run
As the day meets the night.

If It Makes You Happy

Poetry by Nikki Cain, Sophomore
Charcoal by Emily Thomas, Senior

As the twilight fades and the moon begins to rise,
the stars dance across the sky.
They scream your name
and I long for the day
where you will hear their cry.
Your eyes scream like fire,
my envy as green as grass,
but I hold back.
I just want you to be happy,
even if it isn't with me.
Let her know she's lucky
she can hold you in her arms.
I hope she doesn't break your heart...
My storm can rage inside me.
If you're happy, I never want to see you fall apart.
I will do all I can to support you,
and you can talk to me if you ever have a problem.
I will be happy to fix it.
If it makes you happy.
I won't hope to see the end.
I won't be mean or unkind.
As long as I am at least your friend,
This is all I ask for.
Nothing less and nothing more.
If it makes you happy,
Mi amour.

Approval

Poetry Renga by Mariah Rippy, Junior;
Autumn Ladyga, Senior; Ariel Clark, Junior;
and Jacob Hoyt, Junior
Charcoal by Marissa Mills, Junior

She's an ember in my eye,
the girl I used to be.
I only see her in the mirror.
It's because of you I'm no longer me.

I've changed in many ways,
too distant to even know.
What qualities I used to have,
they're too far gone; they do not show.

The ember is slowly burning out;
what will happen when it does?
Am I me
or am I what you always wanted?

I've changed my ways for you;
you don't have a clue.
I'm longing for your approval,
but my attempts are through.

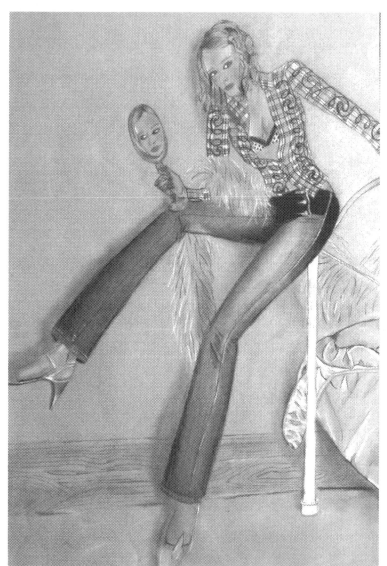

CONTRIBUTORS